GW00832976

A DEᴠɪʟ IN CHARGE?

Notorious Leaders Through the Ages

Helen Walstreaker

Forever In Print Ltd
London

Forever In Print
King Street, London W6

First published in Great Britain 2023

Copyright © Helen Walstreaker 2023

ISBN: 978-1-3999-6941-3

Helen Walstreaker has asserted her right under the
Copywrite, Designs and Patents Act, 1988,
to be identified as Author of this work.

All rights reserved. No part of this publication may be
reproduced or transmitted in any form or by any means ,
electronic or mechanical, including photocopying,
recording, or any information storage or retrieval system,
without prior permission in writing from the publishers.

A DEVIL IN CHARGE?

From Attila the Hun in the first Century AD to Saddam Hussein in the twentieth, "A Devil in Charge ?" looks at what is known about the lives and careers of some of the most ruthless leaders in world history.

CONTENTS

Attila the Hun

Attila the Hun ruled the Hunnic people, a nomadic *people* who lived in Central Asia, the Caucasus, and Eastern Europe, from AD 434 until his death in AD 453. Moreover, he was the leader of a tribal empire in Central and Eastern Europe which included Huns, Ostrogoths, Alans, and Bulgars.

When he was in power, Attila was included amongst the most feared opponents of the Western and Eastern Roman Empires. His armies crossed the Danube twice to plunder the Balkans, but however, they failed to conquer Istanbul, then named Constantinople. Attila's unsuccessful campaign in Persia was followed in AD 441 by a successful invasion of the Eastern Roman Empire which strengthened Attila's confidence to invade the West. Attila also attempted to conquer Roman Gaul (a domain roughly equivalent to modern day France), when he crossed the Rhine in AD 451 and marched as far as Aurelianum (Orléans), where he was brought to a stop at the Battle of the Catalaunian Plains in the Champagne region of Gaul.

Attila later invaded Italy, crushing the northern provinces, but failed to conquer Rome. After planning further campaigns against the Romans, he died in AD 453, but, however, lived on as a character in Germanic heroic legend.

Priscus, a Byzantine diplomat, who wrote in Greek, is a major source for information on the life of Attila and is the only person known to have recorded a physical description of him. The literature and knowledge of the Hunnic people was transmitted orally, by means of epics and chanted poems that were passed down from generation to generation and parts of this oral history have survived via the literature of the Scandinavians and Germans who were neighbours of the Huns and who wrote between

the ninth and thirteeth centuries. Atila is a major character in many Medieval epics including the Nibelungenlied
and various Eddas and sagas.

Attila's Huns were a tribe of Eurasian nomads, originally from east of the Volga river, who migrated further
into Western Europe and built up their sizeable empire
there. The main military techniques they utilized were
mounted archery and javelin throwing. The Huns were
also a society of pastoral warriors whose primary form of
nourishment was meat and milk, these being the products of their herds.

Attila was raised in a speedily altering world. His parents were nomads who had just recently arrived into
Europe. His people had crossed the Volga river during the
370's and annexed the territory of another people, the
Alans, then attacked the Gothic kingdom between the
Carpathian mountains and the Danube. They were a highly
mobile people whose horse-mounted archers had acquired
a reputation for invincibility. Most Germanic tribes were
unable to fight them off.

Large populations fleeing the Huns moved from Ger-
mania into the Roman Empire in the west and south, and
along the banks of the Rhine and Danube. In AD 376, the
Goths came over the Danube River, first of all submitting
to the Romans, but later rebelling against Emperor
Valens, whom they killed in the Battle of Adrianople in AD
378. Moreover, large numbers of Vandals, Alans, Suebi,
and Burgundians crossed over the Rhine and then invaded
Roman Gaul in AD 406 to escape the Huns.

Attila's Huns dominated a large territory with tenuous
borders controlled by the whims of a collection of ethnically diverse peoples. Some were assimilated to Hunnic
society, but many retained their own identities but
acknowledged their king as the king of the Huns. The

Huns were also the indirect source of many of the Romans' problems, driving various Germanic tribes into Roman territory. Relations between the two empires however, remained cordial since the Romans used the Huns as mercenaries against the Germans and even in their civil wars. Because of this, the Roman supplanter, Joannes, was able to recruit thousands of Huns for his army against Valentinian III in AD 424 and it was the Roman general and statesman, Aëtius, who managed this operation.

They made exchanges of ambassadors and hostages in an alliance lasting from AD 401 to AD 450 which aided the Romans in numerous military victories, thus, the Huns had become a great power by the time that Attila had come of age.

The death of Attila's uncle Rugila in AD 434 left his nephews, Attila and Bleda, in control of the united Hun tribes. At this time, the Hun tribes were bargaining with Eastern Roman Emperor Theodosius II's envoys for the return of several renegades who had taken refuge within the Eastern Roman Empire, most probably Hunnic noblemen who had disagreed with Attila and Bleda's assumptions of leadership.

The following year, Attila and Bleda met with the Imperial legation at Margus and negotiated an advantageous treaty. The Romans agreed to return the fugitives, to double their previous tribute of gold, to open their markets to Hunnish traders, and to pay a handsome ransom for each Roman taken prisoner by the Huns. Satisfied with their bargaining, the Huns decamped from the Roman Empire and returned to their home area in the Great Hungarian Plain to consolidate and further strengthen their empire.

Attila stayed outside of Roman attention for the next few years while his Huns invaded the Sassanid Empire.

They were, however, defeated in Armenia by the Sassanids after which they abandoned their invasion, and reverted their attentions back to Europe and in AD 440, they regrouped on the borders of the Roman Empire, making attacks on the north bank of the Danube river.

After crossing the Danube, they overpowered the cities of Illyricum and forts on the river, including Viminacium, a city of Moesia. Their advance began at Margus, where they demanded that the Romans should hand over a bishop who had kept property which Attila regarded as his. While the Romans considered his fate, the bishop secretly slipped away to the Huns and betrayed the city to them.

While the Huns attacked city-states along the Danube, the Vandals, led by Geiseric, captured the Western Roman province of Africa, the richest province of the Western Empire and a main source of food for Rome, and its capital Carthage.

Attila responded with another campaign in AD 443 in which his forces, for the first time, were equipped with battering rams and rolling siege towers, with which they successfully assaulted the military centres of Ratiara and Naissus and massacred the inhabitants.

Making their Advances along the Nišava River, the Huns next captured Serdica, Philippopolis, and Arcadiopolis. Moreover, they encountered and destroyed a Roman army outside Constantinople but were halted by the double walls of the Eastern capital. They also defeated a second Roman army near Callipolis.

The Roman emporer, Theodosius, unable to make effective armed resistance, admitted defeat, and sent his Magister militum per Orientem Anatolius to negotiate peace terms. The terms were harder than the previous treaty: and the Emperor agreed to hand over 6,000 Roman pounds of gold and the annual tribute was tripled and the ransom for each Roman prisoner rose.

Their demands were met for a time, and the Hun kings withdrew into the interior of their empire. Attila then took the throne for himself, becoming the sole ruler of the Huns. In AD 447, Attila rode south again through Moesia into the Eastern Roman Empire. The Roman army, under its magister militum Arnegisclus, met Attila in the Battle of the Utus and the Romans were defeated, although not without inflicting heavy losses. The Huns were then left unopposed and rampaged through the Balkans as far as Thermopylae, northwest of Athens in Greece.

Constantinople itself was saved by the Isaurian troops of magister militum per Orientem Zeno and protected by the intervention of prefect Constantinus, who organized the reconstruction of the walls.

In AD 450, Attila made it known his intent to attack the Visigoth kingdom of Toulouse by making an alliance with Emperor Valentinian III. He had previously been on favourable terms with the Western Roman Empire and its influential general Flavius Aëtius, who had spent a brief exile among the Huns in 433, and the troops that Attila provided against the Goths and Bagaudae had helped earn him the largely honorary title of magister militum in the west.

However, Valentinian's sister was Honoria, who had sent the Hunnish king a plea for help, together with her engagement ring, in order to escape a forced betrothal to a Roman senator. Honoria may not have intended to propose marriage but Attila did interpret her message as such, and accepted, asking for half of the western Empire as dowry. When Valentinian discovered the ruse it was only the influence of his mother Galla Placidia that persuaded him to exile Honoria, rather than kill her. He also wrote to Attila, strongly denying the legitimacy of the supposed marriage proposal. Attila sent an emissary to Ravenna to proclaim that Honoria was innocent, that the proposal had been legitimate, and that he would come to claim what was rightfully his.

The Roman general, Aëtius, made moves to oppose Attila and gathered troops from among the Franks, the Burgundians, and the Celts. A mission by the emperor Avitus together with Attila's continued westward advance convinced the Visigoth king Theodoric I to ally with the Romans. The combined armies reached Orléans ahead of Attila and were able to check and turn back the Hunnish advance. Aëtius gave chase and caught the Huns at a place usually assumed to be near Catalaunum (modern Châlons-en-Champagne). Attila chose to fight the Romans on plains where he could use his cavalry and the two armies clashed in the Battle of the Catalaunian Plains, the outcome of which is usually considered to be a strategic victory for the Visigothic- Roman alliance.

The Visigoth king Theodoric was killed in the fighting, and Aëtius failed to press his advantage. From Aëtius' point of view, the best outcome was what occurred: Theodoric died, Attila was in retreat and disarray, and the Romans had the benefit of appearing victorious.

Attila returned in AD 452 to renew his marriage claim with Honoria and invaded and ravaged Italy along the way. Communities became established in what would later become Venice as a result of these attacks when the residents fled to small islands in the Venetian Lagoon. Attila's army sacked numerous cities and razed Aquileia so completely that it was afterwards virtually unrecognizable as its original site. Aëtius' forces were too under-strength to offer battle, but they managed to harass and slow Attila's advance with only a shadow force. Attila eventually halted at the River Po but, by this point, disease and starvation is believed to have taken a grip in Attila's camp and thereafter hindered his war efforts and contributing to the end of his invasion.

The Roman emperor Valentinian III sent three representatives, who met Attila near the river Mincio in the area of Mantua in Italy and came away from him with the promise that he would withdraw his forces from Italy and negotiate peace with the Romans.

In the Eastern Roman Empire, Emperor Marcian succeeded Theodosius II, and ceased paying tribute to the Huns. Attila withdrew from Italy, while making plans to strike at Constantinople once more to reclaim tribute. However, he died from a knife wound in the early months of AD 453.

Genghis Khan

Genghis Khan was born as Temüjin in approximately the year 1162 in Mongolia, South East Asia. Temüjin had two half-brothers and the siblings grew up in a main camp on the banks of the Onan river, where they learned how to ride horses and use a bow to fire arrows.

When Temüjin was eight years old, his father decided to betroth him to a suitable girl and he took his son to the pastures of the prestigious Onggirat tribe and arranged a marriage between Temüjin and Börte, the daughter of an Onggirat chieftain. Since the marriage would mean that Temüjin's father would gain a powerful ally, and since Börte commanded a high bride price, the chieftain commanded a more powerful negotiating position. He demanded that Temüjin should remain in his household to work off his future bride's dowry. Accepting this condition, Temüjin's father requested a meal from a band of Tatars he encountered while riding homewards alone. The Tatars, however, recognised him as an old enemy and surreptitiously put poison into his food. Temüjin's father gradually got sick but managed to ride back home, where, close to death, he asked a trusted assistant to retrieve Temüjin from the Onggirat, after which he soon died.

Temüjin's father's death broke up the unity of his people and as Temüjin was only about ten years old, and Behter just two years older, neither were thought of as old enough to rule.

Led by the widows of Ambaghai, a previous Mongol chieftain, a Tayichiud faction excluded Temüjin's father from the ancestor worship ceremonies which followed a ruler's death and soon abandoned the camp. A secret history suggests that the entire Borjigin clan followed. All sources agree that most of Temüjin's people renounced his family in favour of the Tayichiuds and that the family was reduced to a much harsher life where they took up a traditional hunter-gatherer lifestyle where they collected roots and nuts, hunted for small animals, and caught fish. As the children grew older, tensions developed since both Temüjin and Behter had claims to be their father's heir: although Temüjin was the child of Yesügei's chief wife, Behter was the senior by at least two years. As the friction intensified, exacerbated by frequent disputes over the division of hunting spoils, Temüjin and his younger brother Qasar ambushed and murdered Behter. Behter's younger full-brother Belgutei, however, did not seek vengeance and became one of Temüjin's highest-ranking followers alongside Qasar.

Also, at around this time, Temüjin developed a close friendship with Jamukha, another boy of aristocratic descent. They exchanged knucklebones and arrows as gifts and swore the anda pact, the traditional oath of Mongol blood brothers, at the age of eleven.

As his family lacked allies, Temüjin was taken prisoner on various occasions, once being captured by the Tayichiuds who had abandoned him after his father's death. Temüjin escaped during a Tayichiud feast and hid first in the Onon river and then in the tent of Sorkan-Shira, a man who had spotted him in the river but not raised the alarm. Sorkan-Shira sheltered Temüjin for three days, at a large personal risk, before allowing him to escape.

Temüjin returned to Dei Sechen to marry Börte when he became considered an adult at fifteen years old. The Onggirat chieftain, happy to see the future son-in-law he feared dead, immediately consented to the union and then accompanied the newlyweds back to Temüjin's camp.

Soon afterwards, seeking revenge for Yesügei's abduction of Hoelun, around three hundred Merkits raided Temüjin's camp and he and his brothers were able to hide on Burkhan Khaldun but both Börte and Sochigel were abducted. Temüjin appealed for aid from a chief named Toghrul and his childhood friend, Jamukha, who had risen to become chief of the Jadaran tribe. Both chiefs were willing to field armies of twenty thousand warriors, and with Jamukha in command, the campaign was soon won. A now-pregnant Börte was rescued and soon gave birth to a son, Jochi, whom Temüjin raised him as his own.

Temüjin and Jamukha camped together for eighteen months during which time they reforged their blood-brother pact, sometimes sleeping together under one blanket. Tensions arose, however, and the two leaders parted, ostensibly on account of a cryptic remark made by Jamukha on the subject of camping and on an active role of Börte in this separation, and whether her ambitions may have been even bigger than Temüjin's own. Whatever the case, the major tribal rulers remained aligned with Jamukha with forty-one named leaders joining Temüjin along with many commoners.

Temüjin was soon acclaimed by his close followers as khan of the Mongols with Toghrul being pleased with his vassal's elevation and Jamukha being resentful. Tensions escalated into open hostility and, in around 1187, the two leaders clashed in battle at Dalan Baljut. The two forces appeared evenly matched, but Temüjin's side was defeated.

In early summer 1196, Temüjin participated in a joint campaign with the Jin against the Tatars, who had begun to exert too much power. As a reward, the Jin awarded Temüjin the honorific cha-ut kuri.

The actions of 1196 fundamentally changed Temüjin's position in the steppe, he was now Toghrul's equal ally, rather than his junior vassal. Jamukha had behaved badly following his victory at Dalan Baljut; it was said he had been beheading enemy leaders and humiliating their corpses and even boiling enemy prisoners alive and a number of disaffected followers defected to Temüjin as a consequence. Temüjin was then able to suppress the disobedient Jurkin tribe that had previously offended him at a feast, refusing to participate in the Tatar campaign. After eliminating their leaders, he had a strong man symbolically break a leading Jurkin's back in a staged wrestling match which contravened Mongol customs of justice, events occurring in 1197.

During the ensuing years, Temüjin and Toghrul campaigned separately and unitedly against the Merkits, the Naimans, and the Tatars. In around 1201, a collection of dissatisfied tribes including the Onggirat, the Tayichiud, and the Tatars, swore to break the domination of the Borjigin-Kereit alliance and elected Jamukha to be both gurkhan and their leader. After some initial successes, this loose confederation was routed at Yedi Qunan, and Jamukha was made to plead for Toghrul's clemency. Temüjin, desiring complete supremacy in eastern Mongolia, defeated first the Tayichiud and then, in 1202, the Tatars. After both campaigns, he executed the clan leaders and took the remaining warriors into his service.

The absorption of the Tatars left three military powers in the Steppe; a belt of grassland that extends some 5,000 miles from Hungary in the west through Ukraine and Central Asia, the Mongols in the east, and the Kereit in between. Seeking to cement his position, Temüjin proposed that his son Jochi marry one of Toghrul's daughters. Led by Toghrul's son Senggum, the Kereit elite believed the proposal to be an attempt to gain control over their tribe. In addition, Jamukha drew attention to the threat Temüjin posed to the traditional steppe aristocracy. Yielding eventually to these demands, Toghrul attempted to lure his vassal into an ambush, but his plans were overheard by some herdsmen. Temüjin was able to gather some of his forces, but was nonetheless defeated at the Battle of Qalaqaljid Sands.

Temüjin retreated southeast to the Baljuna waters, where he waited for his scattered forces to regroup. He called in every possible ally and swore an oath of loyalty, later known as the Baljuna Covenant, to his faithful followers, which would later give them superiority and good standing. These men were from nine different tribes and included Christians, Muslims, and Buddhists united only by loyalty to Temüjin and this group became a model for the later empire.

Soon after, the Mongols caught the Kereit unawares at the Jej'er Heights. The ensuing battle carried on for three days and ended in a decisive victory for Temüjin who sealed his victory by absorbing the Kereit elite into his own tribe. Moreover, he took the princess Ibaqa to be his own wife.

The ranks of the Naimans had grown due to the arrival of Jamukha and others defeated by the Mongols, and they soon prepared for war. In the Battle of Chakirmaut, which occurred in May 1204 in the Altai Mountains, the Naimans were decisively defeated and their leader killed. The Merkits were decimated later that year, while Jamukha, who had abandoned the Naimans at Chakirmaut, was betrayed to Temüjin by companions. Some accounts state that he was then killed through dismemberment. Temüjin was now the sole ruler in the steppe and he held a council at the source of the Onon River in 1206. Here, he formally adopted the title Genghis Khan.

Having gained leadership over one million people, Genghis Khan began what has been termed a "social revolution". Because traditional tribal systems had primarily developed for the benefit of small clans and families, they were not suitable as the foundations for empires. Aware that an alternative structure of organisation would be needed for the functioning of his new nation, Genghis began a series of administrative reforms designed to reduce the strength of tribal loyalties and to replace them with unconditional loyalty to the khan and the ruling family. Since most of the traditional tribal leaders had been killed during his rise to power, Genghis was able to reconstruct the Mongol social hierarchy to his own choices. To break any concept of tribal loyalty, the entirety of Mongol society was reorganised into a decimal system of military organisation. Every man between the age of fifteen and seventy was conscripted into a unit of a thousand soldiers, which was further subdivided into units of hundreds and tens.

From 1206 to 1209, Genghis Khan was predominantly focused on consolidating and maintaining his new nation. During these years, the Mongols imposed their control on surrounding areas. Genghis dispatched Jochi northwards in 1207 to subjugate the Hoi-yin Irgen, a collection of tribes on the edge of the Siberian taiga, and, having secured a marriage alliance with the Oirats and defeated the Yenisei Kyrgyz, he took control of the region's grain trade, fur trade, and gold extraction. Mongol armies also rode westwards, defeating the Naiman-Merkit alliance on the River Irtysh in late 1208. Their khan was killed and his son fled into Central Asia. The Uyghurs pledged themselves to Genghis in 1211 as the first sitting society to submit to the Mongols.

The Mongols had begun raiding the border settlements of the Tangut-led Western Xia kingdom in 1205, rejuvenating the depleted Mongol economy with an influx of fresh goods and livestock. Most Xia fighters were positioned along the southern and western borders of their kingdom to guard against attacks from the Song and Jin dynasties and their northern border relied mostly on the barrier of the Gobi desert for protection. Genghis decided to personally lead a full-scale invasion in 1209.

The Chinese city of Wulahai was captured that May and the Mongols advanced on the capital Zhongxing but suffered a problem fighting against a Xia army. After a two-month stalemate, Genghis broke the deadlock with a successfully executed feigned retreat. At this time Zhongxing was largely undefended but lacking any siege equipment better than crude battering rams, the Mongols were unable to progress with their siege. Genghis' inventive plan to redirect the Yellow River into the city with a dam at first worked, but the poorly-constructed earthworks collapsed and the Mongol camp was flooded, forcing them to retreat. A peace treaty was soonafter put together and the Xia emperor Xiangzong submitted tribute, including his daughter Chaka, in exchange for the Mongol withdrawal.

Wanyan Yongji took over the Jin throne in 1209. He had previously served on the steppe frontier and Genghis greatly disliked him. When asked to submit and pay the annual tribute to Yongji in 1210, Genghis instead mocked the emperor, spat, and rode away from the Jin envoy leaving a challenge which meant war. Since learning of their internal instabilities in 1206, Genghis had made preparations for an invasion of Jin, despite the possibility of being outnumbered eight-to-one by Jin soldiers. He had two aims: to take vengeance for past wrongs committed by the Jin, foremost among which was the death of Ambaghai Khan in the mid-12th century, and to win the vast amounts of plunder his troops and vassals expected.

After calling for a council in March 1211, Genghis launched his invasion of Jin, China that May and reached the outer Jin defense ring during June. These border fortifications were guarded by the Ongud tribe, who were friendly to the Mongols and through his daughter Alakhai Beki, Genghis held an alliance with their leader Alaqush who allowed them to pass without difficulty. The campaign was halted in 1212 when Genghis was wounded by an arrow during the siege of Xijing.

The defenses of Juyong Pass had been strongly reinforced by the time the conflict resumed in 1213, but a Mongol detachment was able to infiltrate the pass and surprise the elite Jin defenders, opening the road to the Jin capital Zhongdu, where modern-day Beijing now stands. The Jin administration began to disintegrate and after the Khitans entered open rebellion, Hushahu, the commander of the forces at Xijing, abandoned his post and staged a coup in Zhongdu, killing his master and installing his own puppet ruler. This governmental breakdown was fortunate for Genghis' forces but, emboldened by their victories, they had seriously overreached and lost their initiative and are reported to have resorted to cannibalism. Genghis opened peace negotiations despite his commanders' objections. He secured reparation, including 3,000 horses, 500 slaves, a Jin princess, and massive amounts of gold and silk, before breaking the siege in spring 1214.

With the northern Jin lands diminished by plague and the Mongols, emperor Xuanzong chose to transfer the capital and imperial court 600 kilometres southwards to Kaifeng. Genghis interpreted this move as a betrayal of the peace treaty and quickly prepared to return home, though he had been away for three years. It was at this time that Genghis decided to fully conquer northern China. His general, Muqali, captured numerous towns in Liaodong during the winter of 1214–1215, and although the inhabitants of Zhongdu surrendered to Genghis at the end of May 1215, the city was sacked and looted anyway. When Genghis returned to Mongolia in early 1216, Muqali was left in command in China where he waged a brutal campaign against the unstable Jin until his death in 1223.

Genghis had now attained complete control of the eastern portion of the Silk Road and his territory bordered that of the Khwarazmian Empire, which ruled over much of Central Asia, Persia and Afghanistan. Merchants from both sides were eager to rescommence trading, which had halted during Kuchlug's rule.

The Khwarazmian ruler Muhammad II dispatched an envoy shortly after the Mongol capture of Zhongdu. Muhammad had grown suspicious of Genghis' intentions, and when Inalchuq, the governor of the Khwarazmian border town of Otrar, decided to halt a caravan, massacre the merchants on grounds of espionage, and seize the goods, the Khwarazmshah turned a blind eye. A Mongol representative was sent to avert war, but he was killed, the killing of an envoy infuriated Genghis, who resolved to leave Muqali with a small force in North China and invade Khwarazmia with most of his army.

Otrar was besieged in autumn 1219, a siege that dragged on for five months, but in February 1220 the city fell and Inalchuq was executed. Genghis had meanwhile divided his forces. Leaving his sons Chagatai and Ogedei besieging the city, he had sent Jochi northwards down the Syr Darya river and another force southwards into central Transoxiana, while he and Tolui took the main Mongol army across the Kyzylkum Desert, surprising the garrison of Bukhara in a pincer movement.

Bukhara's citadel was captured in February 1220 and Genghis moved against Muhammad's residence Samarkand, which fell the following month. Bewildered by the speed of the Mongol conquests, Muhammad fled from Balkh. The two generals pursued the Khwarazmshah until his death from dysentry on a Caspian Sea island in winter 1220/1221.

Genghis' youngest son Tolui was concurrently conducting a brutal campaign in the regions of Khorasan. Every city that resisted was destroyed in a programme of concentrated devastation. This campaign established Genghis' lasting image as a ruthless, inhumane conqueror. Genghis abruptly halted his Central Asian campaigns in 1221, having received news that the disobedient Western Xia had failed to provide Muqali with 50,000 soldiers to campaign against the Jin remnant state in Shaanxi province. Initially aiming to return via India, Genghis realised that the heat and humidity of the South Asian climate impeded his army's skills, while other omens seemed to him unfavourable. Although the Mongols spent much of 1222 repeatedly overcoming rebellions in Khorasan, they withdrew completely from the region to avoid over-extending themselves, setting their new frontier on the Amu Darya river. During his lengthy return journey, Genghis prepared a new administrative division which would govern the conquered territories.

In 1226, immediately after returning from the west, Genghis Khan began a retaliatory attack on the Tanguts. His armies speedily conquered Heisui, Ganzhou, and Suzhou and in the autumn they took Xiliang-fu. One of the Tangut generals challenged the Mongols to a battle near Helan

Mountains but was defeated. In November, Genghis laid siege to the Tangut city Lingzhou and crossed the Yellow River, defeating the Tangut relief army. According to legend, it was here that Genghis Khan reportedly saw a line of five stars arranged in the sky and interpreted this as an omen of his victory.

In 1227, Genghis Khan's army attacked and destroyed the Tangut capital of Ning Hia and continued to advance, seizing Lintiao-fu, Xining province, Xindu-fu, and Deshun province in quick succession in the spring. At Deshun, the Tangut general Ma Jianlong put up a fierce resistance for several days and personally led charges against the invaders outside the city gate. Ma Jianlong later died from wounds received from arrows in battle. Genghis Khan, after conquering Deshun, went to Liupanshan to find cooler weather. The new Tangut emperor quickly surrendered to the Mongols, and the remainder of the Tanguts officially surrendered soon after. Genghis Khan ordered the entire imperial family to be executed, effectively ending the Tangut royal lineage. Genghis Khan died during his final campaign against the Western Xia, falling ill on the eighteenth of August 1227 and dying on the 25th of August 1227, the precise cause of his death remaining a mystery.

Some years before his death, Genghis Khan had asked to be buried without markings and, after he died, his body was returned to Mongolia.

Ivan the Terrible

Ivan Vasilyevich, more usually known in English as Ivan the Terrible, was the first Tsar of Russia from 1547 to 1584. He was the son of a ruler of the Grand Duchy of Moscow and was appointed grand prince after his father's death, when he was merely three years old. When sixteen years old, in 1547, a group of reformers united around the young Ivan and declared him tsar and emperor of all Russia.

During his youth Ivan conquered the khanates of Kazan and Astrakhan and, after he had consolidated his power, he rid himself of the advisers from the chosen council. He then instigated the Livonian War, which ravaged Russia and resulted in the loss of Livonia and Ingria. This did , however, enable him to establish greater autocratic control over Russia's nobility, which he then violently purged with his repressive policy known as the Oprichnina.

Ivan was described as intelligent and devout, but also prone to paranoia, rage, and episodes of mental instability that increased with age. In one fit of rage he murdered his eldest son and heir, Ivan Ivanovich and is suspected to have also caused the miscarriage of his unborn grandchild. This left the politically ineffectual Feodor Ivanovich, his younger son, to inherit the throne, a man whose rule and eventual childless death led to the end of the Rurikid dynasty and the beginning of the Time of Troubles.

Ivan had at least six wives, although only four of them were recognised by the Russian Orthodox Church and he fathered nine children. He was born on the twenty-fifth of August 1530. When Ivan was three years old, his father died from an abscess and inflammation on his leg which developed into blood poisoning. Ivan was proclaimed the Grand Prince of Moscow. His mother Elena Glinskaya initially acted as regent, but she died in 1538 when Ivan was only eight years old, many having thought that she had been poisoned.

On the 16th of January 1547, at age sixteen, Ivan was crowned at the Cathedral of the Dormition of the Moscow Kremlin. Here, were placed on Ivan the signs of royal dignity: the Cross of the Life-Giving Tree, barmas, and the cap of Monomakh. He was also anointed with myrrh, and then he was blessed as the tsar. Two weeks after his coronation, Ivan married his first wife, Anastasia Romanovna, a member of the Romanov family, who became the first Russian tsaritsa.

Other events of the period include the introduction of the first laws restricting the mobility of the peasants, which would eventually lead to serfdom.

The 1560s brought hardships to Russia that led to a dramatic change of Ivan's policies. Russia was devastated by a combination of drought, famine, unsuccessful wars against the Polish–Lithuanian Commonwealth, Tatar invasions, and the sea- trading blockade carried out by the Swedes, the Poles, and the Hanseatic League. Ivan's first wife, Anastasia, died in 1560 and this tragedy badly hurt Ivan and is thought to have affected his personality and also his mental health. At the same time, one of Ivan's advisors, Prince Andrei Kurbsky, defected to the Lithuanians, took command of the Lithuanian troops and devastated the Russian region of Velikiye Luki. On the third of December 1564, Ivan departed from Moscow   for Aleksandrova Sloboda. The remaining boyar court was unable to rule in Ivan's absence and were afraid of the anger of the Moscow citizens and an envoy departed for Aleksandrova Sloboda to beg Ivan to return to the throne, to which he agreed, on condition of being granted absolute power. He demanded the right to condemn and execute traitors and confiscate their estates without interference from the boyar council or church.

He decreed the creation of the oprichnina, a set of wider State policies.

The first wave of persecutions targeted primarily the princely clans of Russia, notably the influential families of Suzdal. Ivan had executed or exiled prominent members of the land-owning clans on trumped-up accusations of conspiracy. In 1566, Ivan extended the oprichnina to eight central districts and of the 12,000 nobles, 570 became imperial police members and the rest were forcibly expelled.

Under the new political system, the imperial police members were given large estates but, unlike the previous landlords, could not be held accountable for their actions. These men took almost everything that the peasants possessed by forcing them to pay in one year what they paid in ten years before. This oppression resulted in more and more incidences of peasants fleeing, thus reducing the overall grain production and increasing the price of grain by around ten times.

Conditions living under the Oprichnina were made worse by an epidemic in 1570, a plague in which up to one thousand people each day died in Moscow. During these difficult conditions with the epidemic, a famine and an ongoing war over Livonia, Ivan grew suspicious that noblemen of the wealthy city of Novgorod were planning to defect and to place the city itself into the control of the

Grand Duchy of Lithuania. In 1570, Ivan ordered the oprichniki to raid the city, which they burned and pillaged together with the surrounding villages, causing the city to never regain its former prominence.

During the massacre of Novgorod, men, women and children were tied to sleighs and run into the freezing waters of the Volkhov River. Ivan had ordered these measures on the basis of non-proven accusations of treason. Other inhabitants were tortured and thousands killed in a pogrom including the archbishop, who was hunted to death.

The Oprichnina did not survive for very long after the sacking of Novgorod. During the Russo-Crimean War of 1571/1572, the oprichniki failed to prove themselves worthy when up against a regular army and in 1572, Ivan abolished the Oprichnina and disbanded his oprichniki.

In 1575, Ivan pretended to resign from his title and proclaimed Simeon Bekbulatovich, a statesman of Tatar origin, to be the new Grand Prince. Bekbulatovich reigned as a figurehead leader for approximately one year and acted under Ivan's instructions to confiscate all of the lands that belonged to monasteries while Ivan pretended not to agree with these decisions. When Ivan re- took the throne in 1576, he returned some of the confiscated land but kept the remainder.

During Ivan's reign, Russia began a large-scale exploration and colonization of Siberia. In 1555, shortly after the conquest of Kazan, the Siberian khan Yadegar and the Nogai Horde, under Khan Ismail, pledged their allegiance to Ivan in the hope that he would help them against their opponents. However, Yadegar failed to produce the full sum of tribute that he had agreed to pay the tsar. Because of this, Ivan did nothing more to protect his inefficient vassal. In 1563, Yadegar was overthrown and killed by Khan Kuchum, who refused to pay tribute to Moscow.

In 1558, Ivan gave the Stroganov merchant family permission to colonise an abundant region along the Kama River and later, lands over the Ural Mountains along the rivers Tura and Tobol. The family also had permission to build forts along the Ob River and the Irtysh River. In around 1577, the Stroganovs engaged the Cossack leader Yermak Timofeyevich to protect their lands from attacks from the Siberian Khan Kuchum.

In 1580, the Cossack leader, Yermak, started his own conquest of Siberia. With over five hundred Cossack fighters, he began to penetrate territories that were controlled by Khan Kuchum and he pressured and persuaded the various family-based tribes to change their loyalties and to become tributaries of Russia. Some agreed voluntarily because they were offered better terms than with Kuchum, but others were coerced. The campaign was successful, and the Cossacks managed to defeat the Siberian army in the Battle of Chuvash Cape. However, Yermak still needed reinforcements. He sent an envoy to Ivan the Terrible with a message that proclaimed the conquered parts of Siberia to now be part of Russia. This was to the dismay of the Stroganovs, who had planned to keep Siberia for themselves. Ivan agreed to reinforce the Cossacks with his armed infantry, but the detachment sent to Siberia perished from starvation without being any help. The Cossacks were defeated by the local peoples, Yermak died and the survivors immediately left Siberia. Ivan died from a stroke while he was playing chess on the twenty-eighth of March 1584 and the Russian throne was left to his middle son, Feodor, a weak-minded figure, who died childless in 1598.

Joseph Stalin

Joseph Stalin was born as Iosif Vissarionovich on the 18th of December 18 December, 1878 He died on the 5th of March, 1953, in Moscow, Russia, U.S.S.R. Stalin was secretary-general of the Communist Party of the Soviet Union from 1922 until 53 and premier of the Soviet state from 1941 until 1953. He ruled the Soviet Union as a dictator for a quarter of a century and transformed it into a major world power. He also industrialized the Union of Soviet Socialist Republics and he forcibly collectivized its agriculture and consolidated his position by using intensive police terror. Moreover, he helped to defeat Germany during the Second World War and extended Soviet controls to include a swathe of Eastern European countries.

As a chief architect of Soviet totalitarianism and a talented, although remarkably ruthless organizer, he dismantled what was the left over of individual freedom but, however, failed to bring about individual prosperity. He did, non-the-less create a mighty military-industrial complex and he led the Russians into the nuclear age.

Stalin was the son of a poor cobbler in the provincial Georgian town of Gori in the Caucasus which was then an imperial Russian colony. Only Georgian was spoken at home but Joseph learned Russian, which he always spoke with a guttural Georgian accent, while attending the church school at Gori from 1888 until 1894. He then moved to the Tiflis Theological Seminary, where he clandestinely read Karl Marx, the chief originator of international Communism, and other forbidden texts. He was expelled in 1899 for revolutionary activity, according to the Communist legend, but left due to ill health, according to his doting mother. His mother, a devoutly religious washerwoman, had hopes of her son becoming a priest. Joseph, however, was more ruffianly than clerical in appearance and outlook. He was only five feet and five inches tall, was stocky, black-haired, fierce-eyed and had one arm longer than the other. Joseph's swarthy face had been scarred by smallpox contracted in his infancy. He was physically strong and endowed with prodigious willpower and he learnt early to disguise his true feelings and to bide his time. In agreement with the Caucasian blood-feud tradition, he was relentless in plotting long-term revenge against those who offended him.

In December 1899, Joseph Stalin briefly became a clerk in the Tiflis Observatory which is the only paid employment that he is recorded as having taken outside of politics. There exists no record of him ever having performed manual labour. In 1900 he joined the political underground and fomented labour demonstrations and strikes in the main industrial centres of the Caucasus. His excessive enthusiasm, however, in pushing unwise workers into bloody clashes with the police did annoy his fellow conspirators.

The Marxist revolutionaries of the Russian Empire split into two competing wings, the Mensheviks and the Bolsheviks in 1903. Joseph Stalin joined the second and more militant, of these factions and became a disciple of its leader, Vladimir Lenin. Between April 1902 and March 1913, Stalin was arrested seven times for revolutionary activity and underwent repeated imprisonment and exile.

Initially, Stalin made slow progress in the Communist party hierarchy. He attended three policy-making assemblies of the Russian Social Democrats, these being in Tampere, Finland in 1905, in Stockholm in 1906 and in London, England in 1907 but at these he made little impression. He was, however, active behind the scenes, helping to plot a spectacular holdup in Tbilisi during June, 1907, in order to raise funds for the party. His first substantial political promotion came in February 1912, when Vladimir Lenin, then in emigration, co-opted him to serve on the first Central Committee of the Bolshevik Party, which had by then split off from the other Social Democrats. During the following year Stalin published, at Lenin's request, an important article on Marxism and the national question. He also briefly edited the newly founded Bolshevik newspaper, Pravda, before he underwent his longest period of exile when he was sent to Siberia from July 1913 until March 1917.

On getting to Petrograd from Siberia in March 1917, Stalin resumed editorship of Pravda. For a shorth while he advocated Bolshevik cooperation with the provisional government of middle-class liberals which had succeeded to power apon the abdication of the last tsar during the February Revolution. However, under Lenin's influence, Stalin quickly switched to the more-militant policy of armed seizure of power by the Bolsheviks. When their coup d'état was carried out in November 1917, his was an important role, but one less strategic than the one played by of his chief rival, Leon Trotsky.

Stalin held two ministerial posts in the new Bolshevik government; he was commissar for nationalities from 1917 until 1923 and for state control from 1919 until 1923. However, it was his position as secretary general of the party's Central Committee, from 1922 until his death, that gave him the power base for his dictatorship. As well as heading the secretariat, he was also a member of the powerful Politburo and of many other interlocking and overlapping committees. He was an arch- bureaucrat who was engaged in quietly outmanoeuvring less brilliant rivals, including Leon Trotsky and Grigory Zinovyev; both of whom loathed this type of mundane organizational work.

From 1921 onward Stalin disobeyed Vladimir Lenin's wishes, until, a year before his death, Lenin wrote a political paper calling for Stalin's removal from his position as the secretary general. Since it came from Vladimir Lenin, the document was potentially the ruination of Stalin's career, but with his frequent luck and his shrewd skill, he managed to have it downplayed during his lifetime.

After Vladimir Lenin's death in January 1924, Stalin promoted an elaborate, quasi-Byzantine cult of the dead leader. Champion of Leninism, Stalin also promoted his own cult in the following year by having the city of Tsaritsyn renamed Stalingrad – it is now named Volgograd. His primciple rival, Leon Trotsky, having previously been Lenin's heir apparent, was now in eclipse after having been ousted by the ruling triumvirate of Zinovyev, Lev Kamenev, and Joseph Stalin. Shortly afterwards, Stalin aligned with the rightist leaders Nikolay Bukharin and Aleksey Rykov in an alliance directed against his former triumvirate cohorts. Putting his hopes into the ability of the Soviet Union to establish a viable political system without there being a worldwide revolution first, the Secretary General advocated a policy of "Socialism in one country". Then his most powerful rivals were all dismissed with Bukharin and Rykov soon following Zinovyev and Kamenev into disgrace and political limbo   pending execution. Joseph Stalin expelled Leon Trotsky from the Soviet Union in 1929 and later had him assassinated in Mexico in 1940. In 1928 Stalin abandoned Lenin's seemingly Capitalist New Economic Policy   in   favour   of   headlong   state-organized industrialization under a series of five-year plans. This had the effect of being a fresh Russian revolution even more destructive in its effects than those of 1917. The dictator's hammer fell most heavily on the peasantry where around twenty five million rustic households were compelled to amalgamate in collective or state farms within a few years. Resisting desperately, the reluctant peasants were attacked by troops and the political police units.

Non-cooperative peasants, termed kulaks, were arrested and shot, exiled, or transferred into the quickly growing network of Stalinist concentration camps, then worked to death under atrocious conditions.

Collectivization created a widespread famine in Ukraine, and Stalin's policies, many of which specifically targeted Ukraine, increased the death and misery. Stalin continued to have grain stocks exported, grain that could have eased the problems in the famine-stricken areas. The famine came to be known as the Holodomor, a combination of the Ukrainian words for hunger and extermination. Some researchers estimate that ten million peasants could have died because of Stalin's policies during that period.

The industrialization policies were less disastrous in their effects, but they too were grandiose failures, to which Stalin reacted by accusing industrial managers of responsibility in a succession of show trials in which they were intimidated into confessing imaginary crimes. The accused were manipulated into serving as self-denounced scapegoats for failures arising from the Stalin's own policies. However, Stalin was surprisingly successful in rapidly industrializing a backward country and this success was widely acknowledged at the time by enthusiastic foreign observers, including Adolf Hitler.

In late 1934, just as the worst excesses of Stalinism seemed to be petering out, the Secretary General launched a new campaign of political terror against the very Communist Party members who had assisted in bringing him to power. His grounds were the December 1st assassination in Leningrad of his leading colleague and potential rival, Sergey Kirov. A suspicion that Stalin himself had arranged Kirov's murder, as an excuse for further mass bloodshed, was greatly hinted at, by Nikita Khrushchev, who was first secretary of the party. This was in 1956 during a speech denouncing Stalin at the 20th Party Congress.

Joseph Stalin used the show trial of leading Communists as a way to expand the new terror. During August 1936, Grigory Zinoviev and Lev Kamenev were paraded in court to repeat fabricated confessions, sentenced to death, and shot. Two more major trials followed in January 1937 and March 1938.

Such were the main publicly acknowledged persecutions that empowered Joseph Stalin to control the Soviet Communist Party and the Soviet elite as a whole. He not only had veteran semi- independent Bolsheviks killed but also many party bosses, military leaders, industrial managers, and high government officials. Others who fell foul of him included foreign Communists on Soviet territory and members of the political police organization, NKVD.

During August 1939, after initially attempting to form an anti- Hitler alliance with the Western powers, Joseph Stalin made a pact with Adolph Hitler, which emboldened the Nazi dictator to attack Poland, which started World War Two.

Concerned about strengthening his frontiers to the West while his new but possibly treacherous German ally was still engaged Westwards, Stalin annexed eastern Poland, Estonia, Latvia, Lithuania, and parts of Romania. He also had Finland attacked and thereby extorted territorial concessions.

In May 1941 Joseph Stalin recognized the increasing danger of a German attack on the Soviet Union and he thus appointed himself chairman of the Council of People's Commissars, his first governmental office since 1923.

Russia's pre-war defensive measures were found to be

weak when the German blitzkrieg broke deep into Soviet territory after Hitler's unprovoked attack on the Soviet Union on the 22nd of June, 1941. Stalin was possibly very shocked by the onslaught, but, none-the-less, he quickly rallied and appointed himself supreme commander in chief. When the Germans got near to Moscow in the winter of 1941, Stalin remained in the threatened capital and helped to organize a powerful counter-offensive. The Battle of Stalingrad, in the following winter, and the Battle of Kursk, in the summer of 1943, were both won by the Soviet Army under Stalin's supreme direction which turned the tide of invasion against the retreating Germans. As war leader, Joseph Stalin held close personal control over the Soviet battlefronts, military reserves, and the war economy.

Joseph Stalin took part in high-level Allied meetings, including those of the "Big Three" with Winston Churchill and Theodore Roosevelt, at Tehrān in 1943, at Yalta and Potsdam in 1945.

After the war ended, Joseph Stalin imposed on eastern Europe a new kind of colonial control similar to Russian Communist regimes which were nominally independent but in reality, they were subservient to Stalin. This way, he increased the number of his subjects by about one hundred million. However, in 1948, the defection of Titoist Yugoslavia from the Soviet camp struck a heavy blow to a plan for world Communism being a Stalin- dominated monolith. To stop other client states from following Tito's example, Stalin instigated local show trials which were manipulated like those of the Great Purge in Russia, which led to satellite Communist leaders confessing to Titoism and many being executed.

After the war, far from continuing his wartime alliance with America and Great Britain, Joseph Stalin now regarded these countries, especially America, as the arch enemy he needed to replace Hitler's Germany.

Back in the USSR, the supremacy of Marxist ideology was harshly reasserted. Andrey Zhdanov, a secretary of the Central Committee, began a reign of terror on the Soviet artistic and intellectual world. Foreign achievements were derided, and the primacy of Russians as inventors and pioneers in practically every field was strongly asserted.

Getting increasingly suspicious and showing signs of paranoia in his later years, Stalin ordered the arrest of many, mostly Jewish, Kremlin doctors on charges of medically murdering various Soviet leaders, including Zhdanov. There is evidence that he was preparing to make this "Doctors' Plot" the pretext for yet another great terror menacing all his senior associates. However, he died suddenly on the 5th of March, 1953, according to the official report.

Adolf Hitler

Adolf Hitler was born in 1889 on the 20TH of April. The birth was in Braunau am Inn, a town in present-day Austria, which was close to the border with the, then, German Empire. He was the fourth of six children born to Alois Hitler and his third wife, Klara Pölzl. Three of Adolf's siblings, however, Gustav, Ida, and Otto, died in infancy. When Adolf was three years old, the family moved to Passau, Germany where he acquired a distinctive lower Bavarian dialect which characterized his speech throughout his life. The Hitler family returned to Austria in 1894, where Adolf attended a state-funded primary school in the municipality of Fischlham.   .

This move coincided with the onset of intense father-son conflicts caused by Adolf 's refusal to conform to the strict discipline of his school. Adolf's father beat him, although his mother attempted to protect him. In 1897 the family moved to a market town called Lambach where the eight-year-old Adolf took singing lessons, sang in the church choir, and even thought about becoming a priest. In 1898 the family returned permanently to the Austrian city of Leonding.

Adolf was deeply affected by the death of his younger brother Edmund, who died in 1900 from measles. Adolf changed from a confident, outgoing, conscientious student to a morose, detached boy who constantly fought with his father and teachers.

Alois had made a successful career in the customs bureau and wanted his son to follow in his footsteps. Adolf later dramatized an episode from this period when his father took him to visit a customs office, depicting it as an event that gave rise to an unforgiving antagonism between father and son, who were both strong-willed. Ignoring his son's desire to attend a classical high school and become an artist, Alois sent Adolf to the Realschule in Linz in September 1900. Adolf rebelled against this decision, and in Mein Kampf states that he intentionally did poorly in school, hoping that once his father saw "what little progress I was making at the technical school he would let me devote myself to my dream".

Like many Austrian Germans, Adolf began to develop German nationalist ideas from a young age. He expressed loyalty only to Germany, despising the declining Habsburg monarchy and its rule over an ethnically variegated empire. Adolf and his friends used the greeting "Heil", and sang the "Deutschlandlied" instead of the Austrian Imperial anthem.

After Alois Hitler's sudden death in January 1903,

Adolf 's performance at school deteriorated and his mother allowed him to leave. He enrolled at the Realschule in Steyr in September 1904, where his behaviour and performance improved. In 1905, after passing a repeat of the final exam, Adolf left the school without any ambitions for further education or clear plans for a career.

In 1907, Adolf left Linz to live and study fine art in Vienna, financed by orphan's benefits and support from his mother. He applied for admission to the Academy of Fine Arts Vienna but was rejected twice. The director suggested Adolf should apply to the School of Architecture, but he lacked the necessary academic credentials because he had not finished secondary school.

In December 1907, Adolf's mother died of breast cancer at the age of forty-seven, when he himself was eighteen. In 1909, Adolf ran out of money and was forced to live a bohemian life in homeless shelters and a men's dormitory. He earned money as a casual labourer and by painting and selling watercolours of Vienna's sights. During his time in Vienna, Adolf pursued a growing passion for architecture and music, attending ten performances of Lohengrin, his favourite Wagner opera. It was in Vienna that Adolf first became exposed to racist rhetoric. Populists such as mayor Karl Lueger exploited the climate of virulent anti-Semitism and occasionally espoused German nationalist notions for political effect. German nationalism had a particularly widespread following in the Mariahilf district, where Adolf lived and Georg Ritter von Schönerer became a major influence on him. He also developed an admiration for Martin Luther. Adolf read local newspapers that fanned prejudice and played on Christian fears of being swamped by an influx of Eastern European Jews. He also read newspapers and pamphlets that published the thoughts of philosophers and theoreticians such as Houston Stewart Chamberlain, Charles Darwin, Friedrich Nietzsche, Gustave Le Bon and Arthur Schopenhauer.

The origin and development of Adolf 's anti-Semitism remains a matter of debate. His friend August Kubizek claimed that Adolf was a "confirmed anti-Semite" before he left Linz. However, historian Brigitte Hamann describes Kubizek's claim as "problematical". While Adolf states in Mein Kampf that he first became an anti-Semite in Vienna, Reinhold Hanisch, who helped him sell his paintings, disagrees. Adolf had dealings with Jews while living in Vienna.

Adolf received the final part of his father's estate in May 1913 and moved to Munich, Germany. When he was conscripted into the Austro-Hungarian Army, he journeyed to Salzburg in 1914 for medical assessment and after he was deemed unfit for service, he returned to Munich. Adolf later claimed that he did not wish to serve the Habsburg Empire because of the mixture of races in its army and his belief that the collapse of Austria-Hungary was imminent.

In August 1914, at the outbreak of World War I, Adolf was living in Munich and voluntarily enlisted in the Bavarian Army. According to a 1924 report by the Bavarian authorities, allowing Adolf to serve was almost certainly an administrative error, since as an Austrian citizen, he should have been returned to Austria. Posted to a Bavarian Reserve Infantry Regiment he served as a dispatch runner on the Western Front in France and Belgium, spending nearly half his time at the regimental headquarters in Fournes-en-Weppes, well behind the front lines. In 1914, he was present at the First Battle of Ypres and in that year was decorated for bravery, receiving the Iron Cross, Second Class.

During his service at headquarters, Adolf pursued his

artwork, drawing cartoons and instructions for an army newspaper. During the Battle of the Somme in October 1916, he was wounded in the left thigh when a shell exploded in the dispatch runners' dugout. Adolf spent almost two months recovering in hospital at Beelitz, returning to his regiment on the fifth of March 1917. He was present at the Battle of Arras of 1917 and the Battle of Passchendaele. He received the Black Wound Badge in May 1918 and in August 1918, on a recommendation by Lieutenant Hugo Gutmann, his Jewish superior, Adolf received the Iron Cross, First Class, a decoration rarely awarded to one of Adolf 's Gefreiter rank.

In October 1918, Adolf was temporarily blinded in a mustard gas attack and was hospitalised in Pasewalk. While there, he learned of Germany's defeat, and – by his own account – upon receiving this news, suffered a second bout of blindness.

Adolf described the war as "the greatest of all experiences", and was praised by his commanding officers for his bravery. His wartime experience reinforced his German patriotism, and he was shocked by Germany's capitulation in November 1918. His bitterness over the collapse of the war effort began to shape his ideology. Like other German nationalists, he believed the Dolchstoßlegende (stab-in-the-back myth), which claimed that the German army, "undefeated in the field", had been "stabbed in the back" on the home front by civilian leaders, Jews, Marxists, and those who signed the armistice that ended the fighting— later dubbed the "November criminals".

The Treaty of Versailles stipulated that Germany had to relinquish several of its territories and demilitarise the Rhineland. The treaty imposed economic sanctions and levied heavy reparations on the country. Many Germans saw the treaty as an unjust humiliation. They especially objected to Article 231, which they interpreted as declaring Germany responsible for the war. The Versailles Treaty and the economic, social, and political conditions in Germany after the war were later exploited by Adolf for political gain.

After World War I, Adolf returned to Munich where without formal education or career prospects, he remained in the army. In July 1919 he was appointed intelligence agent of a reconnaissance unit of the Reichswehr, assigned to influence other soldiers and to infiltrate the German Workers' Party. At a DAP meeting in 1919, Party Chairman Anton Drexler was impressed with Adolf's oratorical skills and gave him a copy of his pamphlet My Political Awakening, which contained anti- Semitic, nationalist, anti-capitalist, and anti-Marxist ideas. On the orders of his army superiors, Adolf applied to join the party and within a week was accepted as a party member.

Adolf made his earliest known written statement about the Jewish question in a September 1919 letter to Adolf Gemlich (now known as the Gemlich letter). In the letter, Adolf argues that the aim of the government "must unshakably be the removal of the Jews altogether". At the DAP, Adolf met Dietrich Eckart, one of the party's founders and a member of the occult Thule Society. Eckart became Adolf's mentor, exchanging ideas with him and introducing him to a wide range of Munich society. To increase its appeal, the DAP changed its name to the National Socialist German Workers' Party, known colloquially as the "Nazi Party". Adolf designed the party's banner of a swastika in a white circle on a red background.

Adolf was discharged from the army in March 1920 and began working full-time for the party. The party headquarters was in Munich, a hotbed of anti-government German nationalists determined to crush Marxism and undermine the Weimar Republic. In February 1921, already highly effective at crowd manipulation, Adolf spoke to a crowd of over 6,000. To publicise the meeting, two truck-loads of party supporters drove around Munich waving swastika flags and distributing leaflets. Adolf soon gained notoriety for his rowdy polemic speeches against the Treaty of Versailles, rival politicians, and especially against Marxists and Jews.

In June 1921, while Adolf and Eckart were on a fundraising trip to Berlin, a mutiny broke out within the Nazi Party in Munich. Members of its executive committee wanted to merge with the Nuremberg-based German Socialist Party. Adolf returned to Munich on the eleventh of July and angrily tendered his resignation. The commit-tee members realised that the resignation of their leading public figure and speaker would mean the end of the party. Adolf announced he would rejoin on the condition that he would become party chairman, and that the party head-quarters would remain in Munich. The committee agreed, and he rejoined the party on the twenty-sixth of July as member 3,680. Adolf continued to face some opposition within the Nazi Party. Opponents of Adolf in the leader-ship had Hermann Esser expelled from the party, and they printed 3,000 copies of a pamphlet attacking Adolf as a traitor to the party. In the following days, Adolf spoke to several packed houses and defended himself and Esser, to thunderous applause. His strategy proved successful, and at a special party congress on 29 July, he was granted absolute powers as party chairman, replacing Drexler, by a vote of 533 to one.

Adolf 's vitriolic beer hall speeches began attracting regular audiences. A demagogue, he became adept at using populist themes, including the use of scapegoats, who were blamed for his listeners' economic hardships.

Adolf used personal magnetism and an understanding of crowd psychology to his advantage while engaged in public speaking. Historians have noted the hypnotic effect of his rhetoric on large audiences, and of his eyes in small groups.

Early followers included Rudolf Hess, former air force ace Hermann Göring, and army captain Ernst Röhm. Röhm became head of the Nazis' paramilitary organisation, the Sturmabteilung (SA, "Stormtroopers"), which protected meetings and attacked political opponents. A critical influence on Adolf 's thinking during this period was the Aufbau Vereinigung, a conspiratorial group of White Russian exiles and early Nazis. The group, financed with funds channelled from wealthy industrialists, introduced Adolf to the idea of a Jewish conspiracy, linking international finance with Bolshevism.

The programme of the Nazi Party was laid out in their 25-point programme on the twenty-fourth of February 1920. This did not represent a coherent ideology, but was a conglomeration of received ideas which had currency in the völkisch Pan-Germanic movement, such as ultranationalism, opposition to the Treaty of Versailles, distrust of capitalism, as well as some socialist ideas. For Adolf, though, the most important aspect of it was its strong anti-Semitic stance. He also perceived the programme as primarily a basis for propaganda and for attracting people to the party.

In 1923, Adolf enlisted the help of World War I General Erich Ludendorff for an attempted coup known as the "Beer Hall Putsch". The Nazi Party used Italian Fascism as a model for their appearance and policies. Adolf wanted to emulate Benito Mussolini's "March on Rome" of 1922 by staging his own coup in Bavaria, to be followed by a challenge to the government in Berlin.

On the eighth of November 1923, Adolf and the SA

stormed a public meeting of 3,000 people organised by Kahr in a beer hall in Munich. Interrupting Kahr's speech, he announced that the national revolution had begun and declared the formation of a new government with Ludendorff. Retiring to a back room, Adolf, with handgun drawn, demanded and got the support of Kahr, Seisser, and Lossow. Adolf 's forces initially succeeded in occupying the local Reichswehr and police headquarters, but Kahr and his cohorts quickly withdrew their support. Neither the army, nor the state police, joined forces with Adolf. The next day, Adolf and his followers marched from the beer hall to the Bavarian War Ministry to overthrow the Bavarian government, but police dispersed them. Sixteen Nazi Party members and four police officers were killed in the failed coup.

Adolf fled to the home of Ernst Hanfstaengl and by some accounts contemplated suicide. He was depressed but calm when arrested on the eleventh of November 1923 for high treason. His trial before the special People's Court in Munich began in February 1924 and Alfred Rosenberg became temporary leader of the Nazi Party. On the first of April, Adolf was sentenced to five years' imprisonment at Landsberg Prison. There, he received friendly treatment from the guards, and was allowed mail from supporters and regular visits by party comrades. Pardoned by the Bavarian Supreme Court, he was released from jail on the twentieth of December 1924, against the state prosecutor's objections. Including time on remand, Adolf served just over one year in prison.

While at Landsberg, Adolf dictated most of the first volume of Mein Kampf at first to his chauffeur, Emil Maurice, and then to his deputy, Rudolf Hess. The book, dedicated to Thule Society member Dietrich Eckart, was an autobiography and exposition of his ideology. The book laid out Adolf 's plans for transforming German society into one based on race. Throughout the book, Jews are equated with "germs" and presented as the "international poisoners" of society. According to Adolf's ideology, the only solution was their extermination. While Adolf did not describe exactly how this was to be accomplished. Published in two volumes in 1925 and 1926, Mein Kampf sold 228,000 copies between 1925 and 1932 and one million copies were sold in 1933, Adolf's first year in office.

Shortly before Adolf was eligible for parole, the Bavarian government attempted to have him deported to Austria. The Austrian federal chancellor rejected the request on the specious grounds that his service in the German Army made his Austrian citizenship void. In response, Adolf formally renounced his Austrian citizenship on the seventh of April 1925.

At the time of Adolf 's release from prison, politics in Germany had become less combative and the economy had improved, limiting Adolf 's opportunities for political agitation. As a result of the failed Beer Hall Putsch, the Nazi Party and its affiliated organisations were banned in Bavaria. In a meeting with the Prime Minister of Bavaria on 4th of January 1925, Adolf agreed to respect the state's authority and promised that he would seek political power only through the democratic process. The meeting paved the way for the ban on the Nazi Party to be lifted that February. However, after an inflammatory speech he gave in February, Adolf was barred from public speaking by the Bavarian authorities, a ban that remained in place until 1927. To advance his political ambitions in spite of the ban, Adolf appointed Gregor Strasser, Otto Strasser and Joseph Goebbels to organise and enlarge the Nazi Party in northern Germany. Gregor Strasser steered a more independent political course, emphasising the socialist elements of the party's programme. The stock market in the United States crashed in October 1929. The impact in Germany was dire: millions were thrown out of work and several major banks collapsed. Adolf and the Nazi Party prepared to take advantage of the emergency to gain support for their party. They promised to repudiate the Versailles Treaty, strengthen the economy, and provide jobs. The Great Depression provided a political opportunity for Adolf. Germans were ambivalent about the parliamentary republic, which faced challenges from right- and left-wing extremists. The moderate political parties were increasingly unable to stem the tide of extremism, and the German referendum of 1929 helped to elevate Nazi ideology. The elections of September 1930 resulted in the break-up of a grand coalition and its replacement with a minority cabinet. Its leader, chancellor Heinrich Brüning of the Centre Party, governed through emergency decrees from President Paul von Hindenburg. Governance by decree became the new norm and paved the way for authoritarian forms of government. The Nazi Party rose from obscurity to win 18.3 per cent of the vote and 107 parliamentary seats in the 1930 election, becoming the second-largest party in parliament.

Adolf made a prominent appearance at the trial of two Reichswehr officers, Lieutenants Richard Scheringer and Hanns Ludin, in late 1930. Both were charged with membership in the Nazi Party, at that time illegal for Reichswehr personnel. The prosecution argued that the Nazi Party was an extremist party, prompting defence lawyer Hans Frank to call on Adolf to testify. On that twenty-fifth of September 1930, Adolf testified that his party would pursue political power solely through democratic elections, which won him many supporters in the officer corps. Brüning's austerity measures brought little economic improvement and were extremely unpopular and Adolf exploited this by targeting his political messages specifically at people who had been affected by the inflation of the 1920s and the Depression, such as farmers, war veterans, and the middle class.

Although Adolf had terminated his Austrian citizenship in 1925, he did not acquire German citizenship for almost seven years. This meant that he was stateless, legally unable to run for public office, and still faced the risk of deportation. On the 25th of February 1932, the interior minister of Brunswick, Dietrich Klagges, who was a member of the Nazi Party, appointed Adolf as administrator for the state's delegation to the Reichsrat in Berlin, making Adolf a citizen of Brunswick, and thus of Germany. Adolf ran against Hindenburg in the 1932 presidential elections. A speech to the Industry Club in Düsseldorf on the 27th of January 1932 won him support from many of Germany's most powerful industrialists. Hindenburg had support from various nationalist, monarchist, Catholic, and republican parties, and some Social Democrats. Adolf used the campaign slogan "Hitler über Deutschland" ("Hitler over Germany"), a reference to his political ambitions and his campaigning by aircraft. He was one of the first politicians to use aircraft travel for political purposes, and used it effectively. Adolf came in second in both rounds of the election, garnering more than 35 per cent of the vote in the final election. Although he lost to Hindenburg, this election established him as a strong force in German politics.

The absence of an effective government prompted two influential politicians, Franz von Papen and Alfred Hugenberg, along with several other industrialists and businessmen, to write a letter to Hindenburg. The signers urged Hindenburg to appoint Adolf Hitler as leader of a government "independent from parliamentary parties", which could turn into a movement that would "enrapture millions of people".

Hindenburg reluctantly agreed to appoint Adolf as chancellor after two further parliamentary elections, in July and November 1932, had not resulted in the formation of a majority government. Adolf headed a short-lived coalition government formed by the Nazi Party (which had the most seats in the Reichstag) and Hugenberg's party, the German National People's Party (DNVP). On the thirtieth of January 1933, the new cabinet was sworn in during a brief ceremony in Hindenburg's office. The Nazi Party gained three posts: Adolf was named chancellor, Wilhelm Frick Minister of the Interior, and Hermann Göring Minister of the Interior for Prussia. Adolf had insisted on the ministerial positions as a way to gain control over the police in much of Germany.

As chancellor, Adolf worked against attempts by the Nazi Party's opponents to build a majority government. Because of the political stalemate, he asked Hindenburg to again dissolve the Reichstag, and elections were scheduled for early March. On 27 February 1933, the Reichstag building was set on fire. Göring blamed a communist plot, as Dutch communist Marinus van der Lubbe was found in incriminating circumstances inside the burning building. At Adolf 's urging, Hindenburg responded by signing the Reichstag Fire Decree of 28 February, drafted by the Nazis, which suspended basic rights and allowed detention without trial. The decree was permitted under Article 48 of the Weimar Constitution, which gave the president the power to take emergency measures to protect public safety and order. Activities of the German Communist Party (KPD) were suppressed, and some 4,000 KPD

members were arrested. In addition to political campaigning, the Nazi Party engaged in paramilitary violence
and the spread of anti-communist propaganda in the
days preceding the election. On election day, 6th of March
1933, the Nazi Party's share of the vote increased to 43.9
per cent, and the party acquired the largest number of seats
in parliament. Adolf 's party failed to secure an absolute
majority, necessitating another coalition with the DNVP..
Having achieved full control over the legislative and executive branches of government, Adolf and his allies began
to suppress the remaining opposition. The Social Democratic Party was banned and its assets seized. While many
trade union delegates were in Berlin for May Day activities,
SA stormtroopers occupied union offices around the
country. On the 2nd of May 1933, all trade unions were
forced to dissolve and their leaders were arrested. Some
were sent to concentration camps. The German Labour
Front was formed as an umbrella organisation to represent all workers, administrators, and company owners,
thus reflecting the concept of Nazism in the spirit of
Adolf's Volksgemeinschaft ("people's community").

In 1934, Adolf became Germany's head of state with
the title of Führer und Reichskanzler (leader and chancellor of the Reich). By the end of June, the other parties
had been intimidated into disbanding. This included
the Nazis' nominal coalition partner, the DNVP; with
the SA's help, Adolf forced its leader, Hugenberg, to
resign on 29 June. On the 14th of July 1933, the Nazi
Party was declared the only legal political party in Germany. The demands of the SA for more political and
military power caused anxiety among military, industrial, and political leaders. In response, Adolf purged
the entire SA leadership in the Night of the Long Knives,
which took place from the 30th of June to the 2nd of July

1934. Adolf targeted Ernst Röhm and other SA leaders who, along with a number of his political adversaries such as Gregor Strasser and former chancellor Kurt von Schleicher, were rounded up, arrested, and shot. While the international community and some Germans were shocked by the murders, many in Germany believed Adolf was restoring order.

On the second of August 1934, Hindenburg died. The previous day, the cabinet had enacted the "Law Concerning the Highest State Office of the Reich". This law stated that upon Hindenburg's death, the office of president would be abolished and its powers merged with those of the chancellor. Adolf thus became head of state as well as head of government, and was formally named as Führer und Reichskanzler (leader and chancellor), although Reichskanzler was eventually quietly dropped. With this action, Adolf eliminated the last legal remedy by which he could be removed from office.

As head of state, Adolf became commander-in-chief of the armed forces. Immediately after Hindenburg's death, at the Instigation of the leadership of the Reichswehr, the traditional loyalty oath of soldiers was altered to affirm loyalty to Hitler personally, by name, rather than to the office of commander-in- chief (which was later renamed to supreme commander) or the state. On the nineteenth of August, the merger of the presidency with the chancellorship was approved by 88 per cent of the electorate voting in a plebiscite.

In early 1938, Adolf used blackmail to consolidate his hold over the military by instigating the Blomberg–Fritsch affair. Adolf forced his War Minister, Field Marshal Werner von Blomberg, to resign by using a police dossier that showed that Blomberg's new wife had a record for prostitution. Army commander Colonel- General Werner von Fritsch was removed after the Schutzstaffel (SS) produced allegations that he had engaged in a homosexual relationship. Both men had fallen into disfavour because they objected to Adolf 's demand to make the Wehrmacht ready for war as early as 1938. Adolf assumed Blomberg's title of Commander-in-Chief, thus taking personal command of the armed forces. He replaced the Ministry of War with the Oberkommando der Wehrmacht (OKW), headed by General Wilhelm Keitel. On the same day, sixteen generals were stripped of their commands and 44 more were transferred; all were suspected of not being sufficiently pro-Nazi. By early February 1938, twelve more generals had been removed.

Adolf took care to give his dictatorship the appearance of legality. Many of his decrees were explicitly based on the Reichstag Fire Decree and hence on Article 48 of the Weimar Constitution. The Reichstag renewed the Enabling Act twice, each time for a four-year period. While elections to the Reichstag were still held (in 1933, 1936, and 1938), voters were presented with a single list of Nazis and pro-Nazi "guests" which carried with well over 90 per cent of the vote. These elections were held in far-from-secret conditions; the Nazis threatened severe reprisals against anyone who did not vote or dared to vote no.

In February 1938, on the advice of his newly appointed foreign minister, the strongly pro-Japanese Joachim von Ribbentrop, Adolf ended the Sino-German alliance with the Republic of China to instead enter into an alliance with the more modern and powerful Empire of Japan. Adolf announced German recognition of Manchukuo, the Japanese-occupied state in Manchuria, and renounced German claims to their former colonies in the Pacific held by

Japan. Adolf ordered an end to arms shipments to China and recalled all German officers working with the Chinese Army. In retaliation, Chinese General Chiang Kai-shek cancelled all Sino- German economic agreements, depriving the Germans of many Chinese raw materials.

On the twelfth of March 1938, Adolf announced the unification of Austria with Nazi Germany in the Anschluss. Adolf then turned his attention to the ethnic German population of the Sudetenland region of Czechoslovakia. On 28–29 March 1938, Adolf held a series of secret meetings in Berlin with Konrad Henlein of the Sudeten German Party, the largest of the ethnic German parties of the Sudetenland. The men agreed that Henlein would demand increased autonomy for Sudeten Germans from the Czechoslovakian government, thus providing a pretext for German military action against Czechoslovakia. In April 1938 Henlein told the foreign minister of Hungary that "whatever the Czech government might offer, he would always raise still higher demands ... he wanted to sabotage an understanding by any means because this was the only method to blow up Czechoslovakia quickly". In private, Adolf considered the Sudeten issue unimportant; his real intention was a war of conquest against Czechoslovakia.

In April Adolf ordered the OKW to prepare for Fall Grün (Case Green), the code name for an invasion of Czechoslovakia. As a result of intense French and British diplomatic pressure, on the 5th of September Czechoslovakian President Edvard Beneš unveiled the "Fourth Plan" for constitutional reorganisation of his country.

Germany was dependent on imported oil; a confrontation with Britain over the Czechoslovakian dispute could curtail Germany's oil supplies. This forced Adolf to call off Fall Grün, originally planned for the 1st of October 1938. On the 29th of September Adolf, Neville Chamberlain,

Édouard Daladier, and Mussolini attended a one-day conference in Munich that led to the Munich Agreement, which handed over the Sudetenland districts to Germany.

Chamberlain was satisfied with the Munich conference, calling the outcome "peace for our time", while Adolf was angered about the missed opportunity for war in 1938; he expressed his disappointment in a speech on 9th of October in Saarbrücken. In Adolf 's view, the British-brokered peace, although favourable to the ostensible German demands, was a diplomatic defeat which spurred his intent of limiting British power to pave the way for the eastern expansion of Germany. As a result of the summit, Adolf was selected Time magazine's Man of the Year for 1938.

In late 1938 and early 1939, the continuing economic crisis caused by rearmament forced Adolf to make major defence cuts. In his "Export or die" speech of 30th of January 1939, he called for an economic offensive to increase German foreign exchange holdings to pay for raw materials such as high-grade iron needed for military weapons.

On the 14th of March 1939, under threat from Hungary, Slovakia declared independence and received protection from Germany.[The next day, in violation of the Munich accord and possibly as a result of the deepening economic crisis requiring additional assets, Adolf ordered the Wehrmacht to invade the Czech rump state, and from Prague Castle he proclaimed the territory a German protectorate.

In private discussions in 1939, Adolf declared Britain the main enemy to be defeated and that Poland's obliteration was a necessary prelude for that goal. The eastern flank would be secured and land would be added to Germany's Lebensraum.

Offended by the British "guarantee" on the 31st of

March 1939 of Polish independence, he said, "I shall brew them a devil's drink". In a speech in Wilhelmshaven for the launch of the battleship Tirpitz on 1 April, he threatened to denounce the Anglo-German Naval Agreement if the British continued to guarantee Polish independence, which he perceived as an "encirclement" policy. Poland was to either become a German satellite state or it would be neutralised in order to secure the Reich's eastern flank and prevent a possible British blockade. Adolf initially favoured the idea of a satellite state, but upon its rejection by the Polish government, he decided to invade and made this the main foreign policy goal of 1939. On the 3rd of April, Adolf ordered the military to prepare for Fall Weiss ("Case White"), the plan for invading Poland on the 25th of August. In a Reichstag speech on 28 April, he renounced both the Anglo- German Naval Agreement and the German–Polish Non- Aggression   Pact.   .

Adolf was concerned that a military attack against Poland could result in a premature war with Britain. His foreign minister and former Ambassador to London, Joachim von Ribbentrop, assured him that neither Britain nor France would honour their commitments to Poland. Accordingly, on the 22nd of August 1939 Adolf ordered a military mobilisation against Poland.

This plan required tacit Soviet support and the non-aggression pact between Germany and the Soviet Union, led by Joseph Stalin, included a secret agreement to partition Poland between the two countries. Contrary to Ribbentrop's prediction that Britain would sever Anglo-Polish ties, Britain and Poland signed the Anglo-Polish alliance on the 25th of August 1939. This, along with news from Italy that Mussolini would not honour the Pact of Steel, prompted Adolf to postpone the attack on Poland from 25th of August to the 1st of September. Adolf unsuccessfully tried to manoeuvre the British into neutrality by offering them a non- aggression guarantee on the 25th of August; he then instructed Ribbentrop to present a last-minute peace plan with an impossibly short time limit in an effort to blame the imminent war on British and Polish inaction.

On the 1st of September 1939, Germany invaded western Poland under the pretext of having been denied claims to the Free City of Danzig and the right to extraterritorial roads across the Polish Corridor, which Germany had ceded under the Versailles Treaty. In response, Britain and France declared war on Germany on 3 September, surprising Adolf and prompting him to angrily ask Ribbentrop, "Now what?" France and Britain did not act on their declarations immediately, and on the 17th of September, Soviet forces invaded eastern Poland.

The fall of Poland was followed by what contemporary journalists dubbed the "Phoney War" or Sitzkrieg ("sitting war"). Hitler instructed the two newly appointed Gauleiters of north- western Poland, Albert Forster of Reichsgau Danzig-West Prussia and Arthur Greiser of Reichsgau Wartheland, to Germanise their areas, with "no questions asked" about how this was accomplished. In Forster's area, ethnic Poles merely had to sign forms stating that they had German blood. In contrast, Greiser agreed with Himmler and carried out an ethnic cleansing campaign towards Poles. Greiser soon complained that Forster was allowing thousands of Poles to be accepted as "racial" Germans and thus endangered German "racial purity". Hitler refrained from getting involved. This inaction has been advanced as an example of the theory of "working towards the Führer", in which Hitler issued vague instructions and expected his subordinates to work out policies on their own.

Another dispute pitched one side represented by Heinrich Himmler and Greiser, who championed ethnic cleansing in Poland, against another represented by Göring and Hans Frank (governor-general of occupied Poland), who called for turning Poland into the "granary" of the Reich. On the 12th of February 1940, the dispute was initially settled in favour of the Göring–Frank view, which ended the economically disruptive mass expulsions. On the 15th of May 1940, Himmler issued a memo entitled "Some Thoughts on the Treatment of Alien Population in the East", calling for the expulsion of the entire Jewish population of Europe into Africa and the reduction of the Polish population to a "leaderless class of labourers". Adolf called Himmler's memo "good and correct", and, ignoring Göring and Frank, implemented the Himmler–Greiser policy in Poland.

On the 9th of April, German forces invaded Denmark and Norway. On the same day Adolf proclaimed the birth of the Greater Germanic Reich, his vision of a united empire of Germanic nations of Europe in which the Dutch, Flemish, and Scandinavians were joined into a "racially pure" polity under German leadership. In May 1940, Germany attacked France, and conquered Luxembourg, the Netherlands, and Belgium. These victories prompted Mussolini to have Italy join forces with Germany on 10 June. France and Germany signed an armistice on the 22nd of June.

Britain, whose troops were forced to evacuate France by sea from Dunkirk, continued to fight alongside other British dominions in the Battle of the Atlantic. Adolf made peace overtures to the new British leader, Winston Churchill, and upon their rejection he ordered a series of aerial attacks on Royal Air Force airbases and radar stations in southeast England. On the 7th of September the systematic nightly bombing of London began. The German

Luftwaffe failed to defeat the Royal Air Force in what became known as the Battle of Britain. By the end of September, Adolf realised that air superiority for the invasion of Britain (in Operation Sea Lion) could not be achieved, and ordered the operation postponed. The nightly air raids on British cities intensified and continued for months, including London, Plymouth, and Coventry.

On the 27th of September 1940, the Tripartite Pact was signed in Berlin by Saburō Kurusu of Imperial Japan, Adolf Hitler, and Italian foreign minister Ciano, and later expanded to include Hungary, Romania, and Bulgaria, thus yielding the Axis powers. Adolf's attempt to integrate the Soviet Union into the anti- British bloc failed after inconclusive talks between Adolf Hitler and Molotov in Berlin in November, and he ordered preparations for the invasion of the Soviet Union.

In early 1941, German forces were deployed to North Africa, the Balkans, and the Middle East. In February, German forces arrived in Libya to bolster the Italian presence. In April, Adolf launched the invasion of Yugoslavia, quickly followed by the invasion of Greece. In May, German forces were sent to support Iraqi forces fighting against the British and to invade Crete.

On the 22nd of June 1941, contravening the Molotov–Ribbentrop Pact of 1939, over three million Axis troops attacked the Soviet Union. This offensive (code-named Operation Barbarossa) was intended to destroy the Soviet Union and seize its natural resources for subsequent aggression against the Western powers. The invasion conquered a huge area, including the Baltic republics, Belarus, and West Ukraine. By early August, Axis troops had advanced 500 km and won the Battle of Smolensk. Adolf Hitler ordered Army Group Centre to temporarily halt its advance to Moscow and divert its Panzer groups to aid in the encirclement of Leningrad and Kiev. His generals disagreed with this change, having advanced within 400 km of Moscow, and his decision caused a crisis among the military leadership. The pause provided the Red Army with an opportunity to mobilise fresh reserves; historian Russel Stolfi considers it to be one of the major factors that caused the failure of the Moscow offensive, which was resumed in October 1941 and ended disastrously in December.

On the 7th of December 1941, Japan attacked the American fleet based at Pearl Harbor, Hawaii. Four days later, Adolf Hitler declared war against the United States.

On the 18th of December 1941, Himmler asked Adolf, "What to do with the Jews of Russia?", to which Hitler replied, "als Partisanen auszurotten" ("exterminate them as partisans").

In late 1942, German forces were defeated in the second battle of El Alamein, thwarting Adolf 's plans to seize the Suez Canal and the Middle East. Overconfident in his own military expertise following the earlier victories in 1940, Adolf became distrustful of his Army High Command and began to interfere in military and tactical planning, with damaging consequences. In December 1942 and January 1943, Adolf 's repeated refusal to allow their withdrawal at the Battle of Stalingrad led to the almost total destruction of the 6th Army. Over 200,000 Axis soldiers were killed and 235,000 were taken prisoner. Thereafter came a decisive strategic defeat at the Battle of Kursk. Adolf Hitler's military judgement became increasingly erratic, and Germany's military and economic position deteriorated, as did Adolf 's health.

Following the Allied invasion of Sicily in 1943, Mussolini was removed from power by King Victor Emmanuel III after a vote of no confidence of the Grand Council of

Fascism. Marshal Pietro Badoglio, placed in charge of the government, soon surrendered to the Allies. Throughout 1943 and 1944, the Soviet Union steadily forced Adolf 's armies into retreat along the Eastern Front. On 6 June 1944, the Western Allied armies landed in northern France in one of the largest amphibious operations in history, Operation Overlord. Many German officers concluded that defeat was inevitable and that continuing under Adolf Hitler's leadership would result in the complete destruction of the country.

Between 1939 and 1945, there were many plans to assassinate Adolf, some of which proceeded to significant degrees. The most well known, the 20th of July plot of 1944, came from within Germany and was at least partly driven by the increasing prospect of a German defeat in the war. Part of Operation Valkyrie, the plot involved Claus von Stauffenberg planting a bomb in one of Adolf 's headquarters, the Wolf's Lair at Rastenburg. Hitler narrowly survived because staff officer Heinz Brandt moved the briefcase containing the bomb behind a leg of the heavy conference table, which deflected much of the blast. Later, Adolf ordered savage reprisals resulting in the execution of nearly five thousand people.

By late 1944, both the Red Army and the Western Allies were advancing into Germany. Recognising the strength and determination of the Red Army, Adolf decided to use his remaining mobile reserves against the American and British armies, which he perceived as far weaker. On the 16th of December, he launched the Ardennes Offensive to incite disunity among the Western Allies and perhaps convince them to join his fight against the Soviets. After some temporary successes, the offensive failed. With much of Germany in ruins in January 1945, Adolf spoke on the radio: "However grave as the crisis may be at this moment, it will, despite everything, be mastered by our unalterable will." Acting on his view that Germany's military failures meant it had forfeited its right to survive as a nation, Adolf ordered the destruction of all German industrial infrastructure before it could fall into Allied hands. Minister for Armaments Albert Speer was entrusted with executing this scorched earth policy, but he secretly disobeyed the order. Adolf's hope to negotiate peace with the United States and Britain was encouraged by the death of US President Franklin D. Roosevelt on the 12th of April 1945, but contrary to his expectations, this caused no rift among the Allies.

On the 20th of April, his 56th birthday, Adolf made his last trip from the Führerbunker (Führer's shelter) to the surface. In the ruined garden of the Reich Chancellery, he awarded Iron Crosses to boy soldiers of the Hitler Youth, who were now fighting the Red Army at the front near Berlin. By the 21st of April, Georgy Zhukov's 1st Belorussian Front had broken through the defences of General Gotthard Heinrici's Army Group Vistula during the Battle of the Seelow Heights and advanced to the outskirts of Berlin. In denial about the dire situation, Adolf placed his hopes on the undermanned and under-equipped Armeeabteilung Steiner (Army Detachment Steiner), commanded by Felix Steiner. Adolf ordered Steiner to attack the northern flank of the salient, while the German Ninth Army was ordered to attack northward in a pincer attack.

During a military conference on 22 April, Adolf Hitler asked about Steiner's offensive. He was told that the attack had not been launched and that the Soviets had entered Berlin. Adolf asked everyone except Wilhelm Keitel, Alfred Jodl, Hans Krebs, and Wilhelm Burgdorf to leave the room, then launched into a tirade against the treachery and incompetence of his commanders, culminating in his declaration—for the first time— that "everything was lost". He announced that he would stay in Berlin until the end and then shoot himself.

By the 23rd of April the Red Army had surrounded Berlin, and Goebbels made a proclamation urging its citizens to defend the city. That same day, Göring sent a telegram from Berchtesgaden, arguing that since Adolf Hitler was isolated in Berlin, Göring should assume leadership of Germany. Göring set a deadline, after which he would consider Adolf incapacitated. Adolf responded by having Göring arrested, and in his last will and testament of 29 April, he removed Göring from all government positions. On the 28th of April Adolf discovered that Himmler, who had left Berlin on the 20th of April, was trying to negotiate a surrender to the Western Allies. He ordered Himmler's arrest and had Hermann Fegelein (Himmler's SS representative at Hitler's HQ in Berlin) shot.

After midnight on the night of 28–29 April, Adolf married Eva Braun in a small civil ceremony in the Führerbunker. Later that afternoon, Adolf was informed that Mussolini had been executed by the Italian resistance movement on the previous day.

On the 30th of April 1945, Soviet troops were within a block or two of the Reich Chancellery when Adolf shot himself in the head and Eva Braun bit into a cyanide capsule. Carrying out Adolf's previous command, their corpses were carried outside to the garden behind the Reich Chancellery, where they were placed in a bomb crater, doused with petrol, and set on fire as the Red Army shelling continued. Grand Admiral Karl Dönitz and Joseph Goebbels assumed Adolf Hitler's roles as head of state and chancellor respectively.

Berlin surrendered on the 2nd of May. The remains of

Joseph and Magda Goebbels, the six Goebbels children, General Hans Krebs, and Adolf's dogs were reportedly buried and exhumed. Adolf Hitler and Braun's remains were alleged to have been moved as well, but this is most likely Soviet disinformation. There is no evidence that any actual bodily remains of Hitler or Braun, with the exception of dental bridges, were found by the Soviets, which could be identified as their remains. While news of Adolf Hitler's death spread quickly, a death certificate was not issued until 1956, after a lengthy investigation to collect testimony from 42 witnesses. Adolf's demise was entered as an assumption of death based on this testimony.

The Holocaust and Germany's war in the East were based on Adolf 's long-standing view that the Jews were the enemy of the German people and that Lebensraum was needed for Germany's expansion. He focused on Eastern Europe for this expansion, aiming to defeat Poland and the Soviet Union and then removing or killing the Jews and Slavs. The Generalplan Ost (General Plan East) called for deporting the population of occupied Eastern Europe and the Soviet Union to West Siberia, for use as slave labour or to be murdered; the conquered territories were to be colonised by German or "Germanised" settlers. The goal was to implement this plan after the conquest of the Soviet Union, but when this failed, Adolf moved the plans forward. By January 1942, he had decided that the Jews, Slavs, and other deportees considered undesirable should be killed.

The victims were killed in concentration and extermination camps, ghettos, and through mass executions. Many victims of the Holocaust were murdered in gas chambers, while others died of starvation or disease or while working as slave labourers. In addition to eliminating Jews, the Nazis planned to reduce the population of the conquered territories by 30 million people through starvation in an action called the Hunger Plan. Food supplies would be diverted to the German army and German civilians. Cities would be razed and the land allowed to return to forest or resettled by German colonists. Together, the Hunger Plan and Generalplan Ost would have led to the starvation of 80 million people in the Soviet Union. These partially fulfilled plans resulted in additional deaths, bringing the total number of civilians and prisoners of war who perished in the democide to an estimated 19.3 million people.

Adolf Hitler's policies resulted in the killing of nearly two million non-Jewish Polish civilians, over three million Soviet prisoners of war, communists and other political opponents, homosexuals, the physically and mentally disabled, Jehovah's Witnesses, Adventists, and trade unionists. Adolf Hitler did not speak publicly about the killings, and seems to never have visited the concentration camps.

The Nazis embraced the concept of racial hygiene. On the 15th of September 1935, Adolf Hitler presented two laws, known as the Nuremberg Laws, to the Reichstag. The laws banned sexual relations and marriages between Aryans and Jews and were later extended to include "Gypsies, Negroes or their bastard offspring". The laws stripped all non-Aryans of their German citizenship and forbade the employment of non-Jewish women under the age of 45 in Jewish households. Adolf Hitler's early eugenic policies targeted children with physical and developmental disabilities and he later authorised a euthanasia programme for adults with serious mental and physical disabilities, now referred to as Aktion T4.

Augusto Pinochet

Augusto Pinochet was a Chilean general and dictator who
ruled Chile from 1973 to 1990, first as the leader of the
Military Junta of Chile from 1973 to 1981, being declared
President of the Republic by the junta in 1974 and becoming the de facto dictator of Chile, and from 1981 to 1990 as
de jure President after a new Constitution, which confirmed him in the office, was approved by a referendum in
1980. His rule remains the longest of any Chilean leader
in history.

   Pinochet rose through the ranks of the Chilean Army
to become General Chief of Staff in early 1972 before
being   appointed its Commander-in-Chief on the 23rd of
August 1973 by President Salvador Allende. On the 11th of
September 1973, Pinochet seized power in Chile in a coup
d'état, with the support of the US, that toppled Salvador
Allende's democratically elected left-wing Unidad Popular
government and ended civilian rule. In December 1974, the
ruling   military   junta   appointed   Augusto Pinochet
Supreme Head of the nation by joint decree, although without the support of one of the coup's instigators, Air Force
General   Gustavo   Leigh.   After   his   rise   to   power,
Pinochet persecuted leftists, socialists, and political critics,
resulting in the executions of between 1,200 and 3,200 people, the internment of as many as 80,000 people, and the
torture of tens of thousands. According to the later
Chilean government, the number of executions and forced
disappearances was at least 3,095. Operation Condor, a
U.S.-supported terror operation focusing on South America, was founded at the behest of the Pinochet regime in
late November 1975, his 60th birthday. Under the influence   of   the   free   market-oriented   "Chicago Boys",
Pinochet's military government implemented economic lib-

eralization following neoliberalism, including currency sta-
bilization, removed tariff protections for local industry,
banned trade unions, and privatized social security and hundreds of state-owned enterprises. Some of the government
properties were sold below market price to politically con-
nected buyers, including Pinochet's own son-in-law. The
regime used censorship of entertainment as a way to
reward supporters of the regime and punish opponents.
These policies produced high economic growth, but critics
state that economic inequality dramatically increased and
attribute the devastating effects of the 1982 monetary crisis on the Chilean economy to these policies. For most of
the 1990s, Chile was the best-performing economy in
Latin America, though the legacy of Augusto Pinochet's
reforms continues to be in dispute. His fortune grew con-
siderably during his years in power through dozens of bank
accounts secretly held abroad and a fortune in real estate.
He was later prosecuted for embezzlement, tax fraud, and
for possible commissions levied on arms deals.

Pinochet's seventeen-year rule was given a legal frame-
work through a controversial 1980 plebiscite, which
approved a new constitution drafted by a government-ap-
pointed commission. In a 1988 plebiscite, 56% voted
against Pinochet's continuing as president, which led to
democratic elections for the presidency and Congress.
After stepping down in 1990, Pinochet continued to serve
as Commander-in-Chief of the Chilean Army until the 10th
of March 1998, when he retired and became a senator-for-
life in accordance with his 1980 Constitution. However,
Pinochet was arrested under an international arrest warrant on a visit to London on the 10th of October 1998 in
connection with numerous human rights violations. Following a legal battle, he was released on grounds of ill-
health and returned to Chile on 3rd of March 2000. In

2004, Chilean Judge Juan Guzmán Tapia ruled that Augusto Pinochet was medically fit to stand trial and placed him under house arrest. By the time of his death on the 10th of December 2006, about 300 criminal charges were still pending against him in Chile for numerous human rights violations during his seventeen year rule, as well as tax evasion and embezzlement during and after his rule. He was also accused of having corruptly amassed at least twenty-eight million US dollars.

Augusto Pinochet was born in Valparaíso, Chile on the 25th of November 1915. In September 1937, he was assigned to the "Chacabuco" Regiment, in Concepción. Two years later, in 1939, then with the rank of Sub-lieutenant, he moved to the "Maipo" Regiment, garrisoned in Valparaíso. He returned to Infantry School in 1940. On the 30th of January 1943, Augusto married Lucía Hiriart Rodríguez, with whom he had five children. By late 1945, Pinochet had been assigned to the "Carampangue" Regiment in the northern city of Iquique. Three years later, he entered the Chilean War Academy but had to postpone his studies because, being the youngest officer, he had to carry out a service mission in the coal zone of Lota. In 1948, Augusto was initiated in the regular Masonic Lodge Victoria n°15 of San Bernardo, affiliated to the Grand Lodge of Chile. He received the Scottish Rite degree of companion, but he is thought not to have ever become a Grand Master.

The following year he returned to his studies in the academy, and after obtaining the title of Officer Chief of Staff, in 1951, he returned to teach at the Military School. At the same time, he worked as a teachers' aide at the War Academy, giving military geography and geopolitics classes. He was also the editor of the institutional magazine Cien Águilas ('One Hundred Eagles'). At the beginning of 1953, with the rank of major, he was sent for two years to the "Rancagua" Regiment in Arica. While there, he was appointed professor of the Chilean War Academy, and returned to Santiago to take up his new position.

In 1956, Augusto Pinochet and a group of young officers were chosen to form a military mission to collaborate in the organization of the War Academy of Ecuador in Quito. He remained with the Quito mission for four-and-a-half years, during which time he studied geopolitics, military geography and military intelligence. At the end of 1959 he returned to Chile and was sent to General Headquarters of the 1st Army Division, based in Antofagasta. The following year, he was appointed commander of the "Esmeralda" Regiment. Due to his success in this position, he was appointed Sub-director of the War Academy in 1963. In 1968, he was named Chief of Staff of the 2nd Army Division, based in Santiago, and at the end of that year, he was promoted to brigadier general and Commander in Chief of the 6th Division, garrisoned in Iquique. In his new function, he was also appointed Intendent of the Tarapacá Province.

In January 1971, Augusto Pinochet was promoted to division general and was named General Commander of the Santiago Army Garrison. On the 8th of June 1971, following the assassination of Edmundo Perez Zujovic by left-wing radicals, Salvador Allende appointed Augusto Pinochet a supreme authority of Santiago province, imposing a military curfew in the process, which was later lifted. However, on the 2nd of December 1971, following a series of peaceful protests against economic policies of Allende, the curfew was re-installed, all protests prohibited, with Augusto Pinochet leading the crackdown on anti-Allende protests. At the beginning of 1972, he was appointed General Chief of Staff of the Army. With rising domestic strife in Chile, after General Prats resigned his position, Pinochet was appointed commander-in-chief of the Army on 23 August 1973 by President Salvador Allende just one day after the Chamber of Deputies of Chile approved a resolution asserting that the government was not respecting the Constitution. Less than a month later, the Chilean military deposed Allende.

On the 11th of September 1973, the combined Chilean Armed Forces (the Army, Navy, Air Force, and Carabineros) overthrew Allende's government in a coup, during which the presidential palace, La Moneda, was shelled and where Salvador Allende was said to have committed suicide. While the military claimed that he had committed suicide, controversy surrounded Allende's death, with many claiming that he had been assassinated.

In his memoirs, Augusto Pinochet said that he was the leading plotter of the coup and had used his position as commander-in- chief of the Army to coordinate a far-reaching scheme with the other two branches of the military and the national police. In later years, however, high military officials from the time have said that Pinochet reluctantly became involved only a few days before the coup was scheduled to occur, and followed the lead of the other branches (especially the Navy, under Merino) as they executed the coup.

The new government rounded up thousands of people and held them in the national stadium, where many were killed. This was followed by brutal repression during Augusto Pinochet's rule, during which approximately 3,000 people were killed, while more than 1,000 remained missing.

In the months that followed the coup, the junta, with authoring work by historian Gonzalo Vial and admiral Patricio Carvajal, published a book titled El Libro Blanco del cambio de gobierno en Chile (commonly known as El Libro Blanco, 'The White Book on the Change of Government in Chile'), in which they said that they were in fact anticipating a self-coup, the alleged Plan Zeta, or Plan Z, that Allende's government or its associates were purportedly preparing. United States intelligence agencies believed the plan to be untrue propaganda. Although later discredited and officially recognized as the product of political propaganda, Gonzalo Vial Correa insists in the similarities between the alleged Plan Z and other existing paramilitary plans of the Popular Unity parties in support of its legitimacy. Pinochet was also trained by the School of the Americas (SOA) where it is likely he first encountered the ideals of the coup.

The US provided material support to the military government after the coup, although criticizing it in public. A document released by the U.S. Central Intelligence Agency (CIA) in 2000, titled "CIA Activities in Chile", revealed that the CIA actively supported the military junta after the overthrow of Allende, and that it made many of Pinochet's officers into paid contacts of the CIA or U.S. military, even though some were known to be involved in human rights abuses. The CIA also maintained contacts in the Chilean DINA intelligence service. DINA led the multinational campaign known as Operation Condor, which amongst other activities carried out assassinations of prominent politicians in various Latin American countries, in Washington, D.C., and in Europe, and kidnapped, tortured and executed activists holding left-wing views, which culminated in the deaths of roughly 60,000 people. The United States provided key organizational, financial and technical assistance to the operation. CIA contact with DINA head Manuel Contreras was established in 1974 soon after the coup, during the Junta period prior to official transfer of Presidential powers to Pinochet; in 1975, the CIA reviewed a warning that keeping Contreras as an asset might threaten human rights in the region. The CIA chose to keep him as an asset, and at one point even paid him. In addition to the CIA's maintaining of assets in DINA beginning soon after the coup, several CIA assets, such as CORU Cuban exile militants Orlando Bosch and Guillermo Novo, collaborated in DINA operations under the Condor Plan in the early years of Pinochet's presidency.

A military junta was established immediately following the coup, made up of General Pinochet representing the Army, Admiral José Toribio Merino representing the Navy, General Gustavo Leigh representing the Air Force, and General César Mendoza representing the Carabineros (national police). As established, the junta exercised both executive and legislative functions of the government, suspended the Constitution and the Congress, imposed strict censorship and curfew, banned all parties and halted all political and perceived subversive activities. This military junta held the executive role until the 17th of December 1974, after which it remained strictly as a legislative body, the executive powers being transferred to Augusto Pinochet with the title of President.

The junta members originally planned that the presidency would be held for a year by the commanders-in-chief of each of the four military branches in turn. However, Pinochet soon consolidated his control, first retaining sole chairmanship of the military junta, and then proclaiming himself "Supreme Chief of the Nation" (de facto provisional president) on the 27th of June 1974. He officially changed his title to "President" on the 17th of December 1974. General Leigh, head of the Air Force, became increasingly opposed to Pinochet's policies and was forced into retirement on 24 July 1978, after contradicting Pinochet on that year's plebiscite (officially called Consulta Nacional, or National Consultation, in response to a UN resolution condemning Pinochet's government). He was replaced by General Fernando Matthei.

Pinochet organized a plebiscite on the 11th of September 1980 to ratify a new constitution, replacing the 1925 Constitution drafted during Arturo Alessandri's presidency. The new Constitution, partly drafted by Jaime Guzmán, a close adviser to Pinochet who later founded the right-wing party Independent Democratic Union (UDI), gave a lot of power to the President of the Republic. It created some new institutions, such as the Constitutional Tribunal and the controversial National Security Council (COSENA). It also prescribed an eight-year presidential period, and a single-candidate presidential referendum in 1988, where a candidate nominated by the Junta would be approved or rejected for another eight-year period. The new constitution was approved by a margin of 67.04% to 30.19% according to official figures; the opposition, headed by ex-president Eduardo Frei Montalva (who had supported Pinochet's coup), denounced extensive irregularities such as the lack of an electoral register, which facilitated multiple voting, and said that the total number of votes reported to have been cast was very much larger than would be expected from the size of the electorate and turnout in previous elections. Interviews after Pinochet's departure with people involved with the referendum confirmed that fraud had, indeed, been widespread. The Constitution was promulgated on 21 October 1980, taking effect on the 11th of March 1981. Augusto Pinochet was replaced as President of the Junta that day by Admiral Merino. During Pinochet's reign it is estimated that some one million people had been forced to flee the country.

Armed opposition to the Pinochet rule continued in remote parts of the country. In a massive operation spear-headed by Chilean Army para-commandos, some 2,000 security forces troops were deployed in the mountains of Neltume from June to November 1981, where they destroyed two MIR bases, seizing large caches of muni-tions and killing a number of guerrillas.

In September 1986, weapons from the same source were used in an unsuccessful assassination attempt against Pinochet by the FPMR. His military bodyguard was taken by surprise, and five members were killed. Pinochet's bul-letproof Mercedes Benz vehicle was struck by a rocket, but it failed to explode and Pinochet suffered only minor injuries.

Almost immediately after the military's seizure of power, the junta banned all the leftist parties that had con-stituted Salvador Allende's UP coalition. All other parties were placed in "indefinite recess" and were later banned outright. The government's violence was directed not only against dissidents but also against their families and other civilians.

The Rettig Report concluded that 2,279 people who disappeared during the military government were killed for political reasons or as a result of political violence. According to the later Valech Report approximately 31,947 were tortured and 1,312 exiled. The exiles were pursued all over the world by the intelligence agencies. In Latin Amer-ica, this was carried out under Operation Condor, a cooperation plan between the various intelligence agen-cies of South American countries, assisted by a United States CIA communication base in Panama. Pinochet believed these operations were necessary in order to "save the country from communism". In 2011, the commission identified an additional 9,800 victims of political repression during Pinochet's rule, increasing the total number of victims to approximately 40,018, including 3,065 killed.

Some political scientists have ascribed the relative bloodiness of the coup to the stability of the existing democratic system, which required extreme action to overturn. Some of the worst cases of human rights violation occurred during the early period: in October 1973, at least 70 people were killed throughout the country by the Caravan of Death. Charles Horman and Frank Teruggi, both U.S. journalists, "disappeared", as did Víctor Olea Alegría, a member of the Socialist Party, and many others, in 1973. British priest Michael Woodward, who vanished within 10 days of the coup, was tortured and beaten to death aboard the Chilean naval ship, Esmeralda.

Many other important officials of Allende's government were tracked down by the Dirección de Inteligencia Nacional (DINA) under the auspices of Operation Condor. General Carlos Prats, Pinochet's predecessor and army commander under Allende, who had resigned rather than support the moves against Allende's government, was assassinated in Buenos Aires, Argentina, in 1974. A year later, the murder of 119 opponents abroad was disguised as an internal conflict, the DINA setting up a propaganda campaign to support this idea (Operation Colombo), a campaign publicised by the leading newspaper in Chile, El Mercurio.

Other victims of Condor included Juan José Torres, the former President of Bolivia, assassinated in Buenos Aires on the 2nd of June 1976; Carmelo Soria, a UN diplomat working for the CEPAL, assassinated in July 1976; and Orlando Letelier, a former Chilean ambassador to the United States and minister in Allende's cabinet, assassinated after his release from internment and exile in Washington, D.C. by a car bomb on the 21st of September 1976. Documents confirm that Augusto Pinochet directly

ordered Letelier's assassination. This led to strained relations with the US and to the extradition of Michael Townley, a US citizen who worked for the DINA and had
organized Letelier's assassination. Other targeted victims,
who escaped assassination, included Christian-Democrat
Bernardo Leighton, who escaped an assassination attempt
in Rome in 1975 by the Italian terrorist Stefano delle Chi-
aie; Carlos Altamirano, the leader of the Chilean Socialist
Party, targeted for murder in 1975 by Augusto Pinochet,
along with Volodia Teitelboim, member of the Communist
Party; Pascal Allende, the nephew of Salvador Allende and
president of the MIR, who escaped an assassination
attempt in Costa Rica in March 1976; and US Congress-
man Edward Koch, who became aware in 2001 of relations
between death threats and his denunciation of Operation
Condor. Furthermore, according to later investigations,
Eduardo Frei Montalva, the Christian Democrat President
of Chile from 1964 to 1970, may have been poisoned in
1982 with toxins produced by DINA biochemist Eugenio
Berrios.

Protests continued, however, during the 1980s, lead-
ing to several scandals. In March 1985, the murder of three
Communist Party members led to the resignation of César
Mendoza, head of the Carabineros and member of the
junta since its formation. During a 1986 protest against
Pinochet, 21-year-old American photographer Rodrigo
Rojas DeNegri and 18-year-old student Carmen Gloria
Quintana were burnt alive, with only Carmen surviving.

In August 1989, Marcelo Barrios Andres, a 21-year-old
member of the FPMR (the armed wing of the PCC, created
in 1983, which had attempted to assassinate Pinochet on
the 7th of September 1986), was murdered by a group of
military personnel who were supposed to arrest him
on orders of Valparaíso's public prosecutor. This case was

included in the Rettig Report. Among the killed and disappeared during the military junta were 440 MIR guerrillas. In December 2015, three former DINA agents were sentenced to ten years in prison for the murder of a 29-year-old theology student and activist, German Rodriguez Cortes, in 1978. The same month, 62-year-old Guillermo Reyes Rammsy, a former Chilean soldier during the Pinochet years, was arrested and charged with murder for boasting of participating in 18 executions during a live phone-in to the Chilean radio show "Chacotero Sentimental".

Pinochet's regime was responsible for many human rights abuses during its reign, including forced disappearances, murder, and torture of political opponents. According to a government commission report that included testimony from more than 30,000 people, Augusto Pinochet's government killed at least 3,197 people and tortured about 29,000. Two-thirds of the cases listed in the report happened in 1973.

The renowned Chilean singer, theatre director and academic Víctor Jara was found in a dirty canal "with his hands and face extremely disfigured" and with "forty-four bullet holes". Moreover, the practice of murdering political opponents via "death flights", employed by the juntas of Argentina and Chile, has sometimes been the subject of numerous alt-right and other right-wing extremist groups internet memes, with the suggestion that political enemies and leftists be given "free helicopter rides". In 2001, Chilean President Ricardo Lagos informed the nation that during Augusto Pinochet's reign, 120 bodies had been tossed from helicopters into "the ocean, the lakes and the rivers of Chile". In a final assessment of his legacy during his funeral, Belisario Velasco, Chile's interior minister at the time remarked that " Pinochet was a classic right-wing dictator who badly violated human rights and who became rich."

During the 1990s, while no longer President still commander- in-chief, Pinochet scoffed at his human rights critics. When asked about the discovery of a mass grave of his government's victims, Augusto Pinochet was quoted in the Chilean press as joking that it was an "efficient" way of burial.

Augusto Pinochet and his government have been characterised as fascist. For example, journalist and author Samuel Chavkin, in his book Storm Over Chile: The Junta Under Siege, repeatedly characterizes both Pinochet himself and the military dictatorship as fascist.

Pinochet was arrested in London on "charges of genocide and terrorism that include murder" in October 1998. The indictment and arrest of Pinochet was the first time that a former government head was arrested on the principle of universal jurisdiction.

After having been placed under house arrest on the grounds of the Wentworth Club in Britain in October 1998 and initiating a judicial and public relations battle, the latter run by Thatcherite political operative Patrick Robertson, he was released in March 2000 on medical grounds by the Home Secretary Jack Straw without facing trial. Straw had overruled a House of Lords decision to extradite Pinochet to face trial in Spain.

Pinochet returned to Chile on the 3rd of March 2000. So as to avoid any potential disruption his flight back to Chile from the UK departed from RAF Waddington, evading those protesting against his release. His first act when landing in Santiago's airport was to triumphantly get up from his wheelchair to the acclaim of his supporters. He was greeted by his successor as head of the Chilean armed forces, General Ricardo Izurieta. Ricardo Lagos said the retired general's televised arrival had damaged the image of Chile, while thousands demon-strated against him.

The Supreme Court ruled in favor of judge Juan Guzmán's request in August 2000, and Augusto Pinochet was indicted on the 1st of December 2000 for the kidnap-ping of 75 opponents in the Caravan of Death case. Guzmán advanced the charge of kidnapping as the 75 were officially "disappeared": even though they were all most likely dead, the absence of their corpses made any charge of "homicide" difficult.

In July 2002, the Supreme Court dismissed Pinochet's indictment in the various human rights abuse cases, for medical reasons (vascular dementia). The debate concerned Pinochet's mental faculties, his legal team claiming that he was senile and could not remember, while others (including several physicians) claimed that he was affected only physically but retained all control of his faculties. The same year, the prosecuting attorney Hugo Guttierez, in charge of the Caravan of Death case, declared, "Our country has the degree of justice that the political transition permits us to have."

Pinochet resigned from his senatorial seat shortly after the Supreme Court's July 2002 ruling. In May 2004, the Supreme Court overturned its precedent decision, and ruled that he was capable of standing trial. In arguing their case, the prosecution presented a recent TV interview Pinochet had given to journalist Maria Elvira Salazar for a Miami-based television network, which raised doubts about his alleged mental incapacity. In December 2004, he was charged with several crimes, including the 1974 assassina-tion of General Prats and the Operation Colombo case in which 119 died, and was again placed under house arrest. He suffered a stroke on the 18th of December 2004. Ques-tioned by his judges in order to know if, as president, he was the direct head of DINA, he answered: "I don't remember, but it's not true. And if it were true, I don't remember."

In January 2005, the Chilean Army accepted institutional responsibility for past human rights abuses. In 2006, Pinochet was indicted for kidnappings and torture at the Villa Grimaldi detention center by judge Alejandro Madrid (Guzmán's successor), as well as for the 1995 assassination of the DINA biochemist Eugenio Berrios, himself involved in the Letelier case. Berrios, who had worked with Michael Townley, had produced sarin, anthrax and botulism in the Bacteriological War Army Laboratory for Pinochet; these materials were used against political opponents. The DINA biochemist was also alleged to have created black cocaine, which Augusto Pinochet then sold in Europe and the United States. The money for the drug trade was allegedly deposited into Pinochet's bank accounts. On the 25th of November 2006, Augusto Pinochet marked his 91st birthday by having his wife read a statement he had written to admirers present for his birthday:

> *"Today, near the end of my days, I want to say that I harbour no rancour against anybody, that I love my fatherland above all and that I take political responsibility for everything that was done which had no other goal than making Chile greater and avoiding its disintegration ... I assume full political responsibility for what happened."*

Two days later, he was again indicted and ordered preliminary house arrest on charges of kidnapping and murder of two bodyguards of Salvador Allende who were arrested the day of the 1973 coup and executed by firing squad during the Caravan of Death.

Augusto Pinochet died a few days later, on the 10th of December 2006, without having been convicted of any of the crimes of which he was accused. He suffered a heart attack on the morning of the 3rd of December 2006 and was given the last rites the same day. On the next day the Chilean Court of Appeals ordered the suspension of his house arrest. On the 10th of December 2006 he was taken to the intensive care unit and died of congestive heart failure and pulmonary edema, surrounded by family members, at the Military Hospital.

Chairman Mao

Mao Zedong, also known as Chairman Mao, was a Chinese communist revolutionary who was the founder of the People's Republic of China (PRC), which he led as the chairman of the Chinese Communist Party from the establishment of the PRC in 1949 until his death in 1976. Ideologically a Marxist–Leninist, his theories, military strategies, and political policies are collectively known as Maoism.

Mao was the son of a prosperous peasant in Shaoshan, Hunan. He supported Chinese nationalism and had an anti-imperialist outlook early in his life, and was particularly influenced by the events of the Xinhai Revolution of 1911 and May Fourth Movement of 1919. He later adopted Marxism–Leninism while working at Peking University as a librarian and became a founding member of the Chinese Communist Party (CCP), leading the Autumn Harvest Uprising in 1927. During the Chinese Civil War between the Kuomintang (KMT) and the CCP, Mao helped to found the Chinese Workers' and Peasants' Red Army, led the Jiangxi Soviet's radical land reform policies, and ultimately became head of the CCP during the Long March. Although the CCP temporarily allied with the KMT under the Second United Front during the Second Sino-Japanese War (1937–1945), China's civil war resumed after Japan's surrender, and Mao's forces defeated the Nationalist government, which withdrew to Taiwan in 1949.

On the 1st of October 1949, Mao proclaimed the foundation of the PRC, a Marxist–Leninist single-party state controlled by the CCP. In the following years he solidified his control through the Chinese Land Reform against landlords, the Campaign to Suppress Counterrevolutionaries, the "Three-anti and Five-anti Campaigns", and through a truce in the Korean War, which altogether resulted in the deaths of several million Chinese. From 1953 to 1958, Mao played an important role in enforcing command economy in China, constructing the first Constitution of the PRC, launching the industrialisation program, and initiating military projects such as the "Two Bombs, One Satellite" project and Project 523. His foreign policies during this time were dominated by the Sino-Soviet split which drove a wedge between China and the Soviet Union. In 1955, Mao launched the Sufan movement, and in 1957 he launched the Anti-Rightist Campaign, in which at least 550,000 people, mostly intellectuals and dissidents, were persecuted. In 1958, he launched the Great Leap Forward that aimed to rapidly transform China's economy from agrarian to industrial, which led to the deadliest famine in history and the deaths of 15–55 million people between 1958 and 1962. In 1963, Mao launched the Socialist Education Movement, and in 1966 he initiated the Cultural Revolution, a program to remove counter- revolutionary" elements in Chinese society which lasted 10 years and was marked by violent class struggle, widespread destruction of cultural artifacts, and an unprecedented elevation of Mao's cult of personality. Tens of millions of people were persecuted during the Revolution, while the estimated number of deaths ranges from hundreds of thousands to millions. After years of ill health, Mao suffered a series of heart attacks in 1976 and died at the age of 82. During Mao's era, China's population grew from around 550 million to over 900 million while the government did not strictly enforce its family planning policy. Widely regarded as one of the most influential figures of the twentieth century, Mao remains a controversial figure within and outside China. The government during Mao's rule was also responsible for vast numbers of deaths, with estimates ranging from forty to eighty million victims through starvation, persecution, prison labour, and mass executions. During his leadership tenure, China was heavily involved with other Asian communist conflicts such as the Korean War, the Vietnam War, and the Cambodian Civil War, which brought the Khmer Rouge to power. Beyond politics, Mao is also known as a theorist, military strategist, and poet. Mao has been praised for transforming China from a semi-colony to a leading world power, with greatly advanced literacy, women's rights, basic healthcare, primary education and life expectancy.

Mao Zedong was born on the 26th of December 1893, in Shaoshan village, Hunan. His father, Mao Yichang, was a formerly impoverished peasant who had become one of the wealthiest farmers in Shaoshan. Growing up in rural Hunan, Mao described his father as a stern disciplinarian, who would beat him and his three siblings, the boys Zemin and Zetan, as well as an adopted girl, Zejian. Mao's mother, Wen Qimei, was a devout Buddhist who tried to temper her husband's strict attitude. Mao too became a

Buddhist, but abandoned this faith in his mid-teenage years. At age eight, Mao was sent to Shaoshan Primary School. Learning the value systems of Confucianism, he later admitted that he did not enjoy the classical Chinese texts preaching Confucian morals, instead favouring classic novels like Romance of the Three Kingdoms and Water Margin. At age thirteen, Mao finished primary education, and his father united him in an arranged marriage to the 17-year-old Luo Yixiu, thereby uniting their land-owning families. Mao refused to recognise her as his wife, becoming a fierce critic of arranged marriage and temporarily moving away. Luo was locally disgraced and died in 1910, at only twenty-one years of age.

While working on his father's farm, Mao read voraciously and developed a "political consciousness" from Zheng Guanying's booklet which lamented the deterioration of Chinese power and argued for the adoption of representative democracy. Interested in history, Mao was inspired by the military prowess and nationalistic fervour of George Washington and Napoleon Bonaparte. His political views were shaped by Gelaohui-led protests which erupted following a famine in Changsha, the capital of Hunan; Mao supported the protesters' demands, but the armed forces suppressed the dissenters and executed their leaders. The famine spread to Shaoshan, where starving peasants seized his father's grain. He disapproved of their actions as morally wrong, but claimed sympathy for their situation. At age sixteen, Mao moved to a higher primary school in nearby Dongshan where he was bullied for his peasant background.

In 1911, Mao began middle school in Changsha. Revolutionary sentiment was strong in the city, where there was widespread animosity towards Emperor Puyi's absolute monarchy and many were advocating republicanism.

The republicans' figurehead was Sun Yat-sen, an American-educated Christian who led the Tongmenghui society. In Changsha, Mao was influenced by Sun's newspaper, The People's Independence (Minli bao), and called for Sun to become president in a school essay. As a symbol of rebellion against the Manchu monarch, Mao and a friend cut off their queue pigtails, a sign of subservience to the emperor.

Inspired by Sun's republicanism, the army rose up across southern China, sparking the Xinhai Revolution. Changsha's governor fled, leaving the city in republican control. Supporting the revolution, Mao joined the rebel army as a private soldier, but was not involved in fighting. The northern provinces remained loyal to the emperor, and hoping to avoid a civil war, Sun—proclaimed "provisional president" by his supporters, compromised with the monarchist general Yuan Shikai. The monarchy was abolished, creating the Republic of China, but the monarchist Yuan became president. The revolution over, Mao resigned from the army in 1912, after six months as a soldier. Around this time, Mao discovered socialism from a newspaper article; proceeding to read pamphlets by Jiang Kanghu, the student founder of the Chinese Socialist Party, Mao remained interested yet unconvinced by the idea.

Over the next few years, Mao enrolled and dropped out of a police academy, a soap-production school, a law school, an economics school, and the government-run Changsha Middle School. Studying independently, he spent much time in Changsha's library, reading core works of classical liberalism such as Adam Smith's The Wealth of Nations and Montesquieu's The Spirit of the Laws, as well as the works of western scientists and philosophers such as Darwin, Mill, Rousseau, and Spencer. Viewing himself as an intellectual, years later he admitted that at this time he thought himself better than working people. He was inspired by Friedrich Paulsen, a neo-Kantian philosopher and educator whose emphasis on the achievement of a carefully defined goal as the highest value led Mao to believe that strong individuals were not bound by moral codes but should strive for a great goal. His father saw no use in his son's intellectual pursuits, cut off his allowance and forced him to move into a hostel for the destitute.

Mao desired to become a teacher and enrolled at the Fourth Normal School of Changsha, which soon merged with the First Normal School of Hunan, widely seen as the best in Hunan. Befriending Mao, professor Yang Changji urged him to read a radical newspaper, New Youth (Xin qingnian), the creation of his friend Chen Duxiu, a dean at Peking University. Although he was a supporter of Chinese nationalism, Chen argued that China must look to the west to cleanse itself of superstition and autocracy. In his first school year, Mao befriended an older student, Xiao Zisheng; together they went on a walking tour of Hunan, begging and writing literary couplets to obtain food.

A popular student, in 1915 Mao was elected secretary of the Students Society. He organised the Association for Student Self- Government and led protests against school rules. Mao published his first article in New Youth in April 1917, instructing readers to increase their physical strength to serve the revolution. He joined the Society for the Study of Wang Fuzhi (Chuan-shan Hsüeh-she), a revolutionary group founded by Changsha literati who wished to emulate the philosopher Wang Fuzhi. In spring 1917, he was elected to command the students' volunteer army, set up to defend the school from marauding soldiers. Increasingly interested in the techniques of war, he took a keen interest in World War I, and also began to develop a sense of solidarity with workers. Mao undertook feats of physical endurance with Xiao Zisheng and Cai Hesen, and with other young revolutionaries they formed the Renovation of the People Study Society in April 1918 to debate Chen Duxiu's ideas. Desiring personal and societal transformation, the Society gained 70–80 members, many of whom would later join the Communist Party. Mao graduated in June 1919, ranked third in the year.

Mao moved to Beijing, where his mentor Yang Changji had taken a job at Peking University. Yang thought Mao exceptionally "intelligent and handsome", securing him a job as assistant to the university librarian Li Dazhao, who would become an early Chinese Communist. Li authored a series of New Youth articles on the October Revolution in Russia, during which the Communist Bolshevik Party under the leadership of Vladimir Lenin had seized power. Lenin was an advocate of the socio- political theory of Marxism, first developed by the German sociologists Karl Marx and Friedrich Engels, and Li's articles added Marxism to the doctrines in Chinese revolutionary movement.

Becoming "more and more radical", Mao was initially influenced by Peter Kropotkin's anarchism, which was the most prominent radical doctrine of the day. Chinese anarchists, such as Cai Yuanpei, Chancellor of Peking University, called for complete social revolution in social relations, family structure, and women's equality, rather than the simple change in the form of government called for by earlier revolutionaries. He joined Li's Study Group and "developed rapidly toward Marxism" during the winter of 1919. Paid a low wage, Mao lived in a cramped room with seven other Hunanese students, but believed that Beijing's beauty offered "vivid and living compensation". A number of his friends took advantage of the anarchist-organised Mouvement Travail-Études to study in France, but Mao declined, perhaps because of an inability to learn languages.

At the university, Mao was snubbed by other students due to his rural Hunanese accent and lowly position. He joined the university's Philosophy and Journalism Societies and attended lectures and seminars by the likes of Chen Duxiu, Hu Shih, and Qian Xuantong. Mao's time in Beijing ended in the spring of 1919, when he travelled to Shanghai with friends who were preparing to leave for France. He did not return to Shaoshan, where his mother was terminally ill. She died in October 1919 and her husband died in January 1920.

On the 4th of May 1919, students in Beijing gathered at the Tiananmen to protest the Chinese government's weak resistance to Japanese expansion in China. Patriots were outraged at the influence given to Japan in the Twenty-One Demands in 1915, the complicity of Duan Qirui's Beiyang Government, and the betrayal of China in the Treaty of Versailles, wherein Japan was allowed to receive territories in Shandong which had been surrendered by Germany. These demonstrations ignited the nationwide May Fourth Movement and fuelled the New Culture Movement which blamed China's diplomatic defeats on social and cultural backwardness.

In Changsha, Mao had begun teaching history at the Xiuye Primary School and organising protests against the pro-Duan Governor of Hunan Province, Zhang Jingyao, popularly known as "Zhang the Venomous" due to his corrupt and violent rule. In late May, Mao co-founded the Hunanese Student Association with He Shuheng and Deng Zhongxia, organising a student strike for June and in July 1919 began production of a weekly radical magazine, Xiang River Review. Using vernacular language that would be understandable to the majority of China's populace, he advocated the need for a "Great Union of the Popular Masses", strengthened trade unions able to wage non-violent revolution. His ideas were not Marxist, but heavily influenced by Kropotkin's concept of mutual aid.

Zhang banned the Student Association, but Mao continued publishing after assuming editorship of the liberal magazine New Hunan (Xin Hunan) and offered articles in popular local newspaper Ta Kung Pao. Several of these advocated feminist views, calling for the liberation of women in Chinese society; Mao was influenced by his forced arranged-marriage. In fall 1919, Mao organized a seminar in Changsha studying economic and political issues, as well as ways to unite the people, the feasibility of socialism, and issues regarding Confucianism.

During this period, Mao involved himself in political work with manual laborers, setting up night schools and trade unions. In December 1919, Mao helped organise a general strike in Hunan, securing some concessions, but Mao and other student leaders felt threatened by Zhang, and Mao returned to Beijing, visiting the terminally ill Yang Changji. Mao found that his articles had achieved a level of fame among the revolutionary movement, and set about soliciting support in overthrowing Zhang. Coming across newly translated Marxist literature by Thomas Kirkup, Karl Kautsky, and Marx and Engels—notably The Communist Manifesto—he came under their increasing influence, but was still eclectic in his views.

Mao visited Tianjin, Jinan, and Qufu, before moving to Shanghai, where he worked as a laundryman and met Chen Duxiu, noting that Chen's adoption of Marxism "deeply impressed me at what was probably a critical period in my life". In Shanghai, Mao met an old teacher of his, Yi Peiji, a revolutionary and member of the Kuomintang (KMT), or Chinese Nationalist Party, which was gaining increasing support and influence. Yi introduced Mao to General Tan Yankai, a senior KMT member who held the loyalty of troops stationed along the Hunanese border with Guangdong. Tan was plotting to overthrow Zhang, and Mao aided him by organising the Changsha students. In June 1920, Tan led his troops into Changsha, and Zhang fled. In the subsequent reorganisation of the provincial administration, Mao was appointed headmaster of the junior section of the First Normal School. Now receiving a large income, he married Yang Kaihui, daughter of Yang Changji, in the winter of 1920.

The Chinese Communist Party was founded by Chen Duxiu and Li Dazhao in the French concession of Shanghai in 1921 as a study society and informal network. Mao set up a Changsha branch, also establishing a branch of the Socialist Youth Corps and a Cultural Book Society which opened a bookstore to propagate revolutionary literature throughout Hunan. He was involved in the movement for Hunan autonomy, in the hope that a Hunanese constitution would increase civil liberties and make his revolutionary activity easier. When the movement was successful in establishing provincial autonomy under a new warlord, Mao forgot his involvement. By 1921, small Marxist groups existed in Shanghai, Beijing, Changsha, Wuhan, Guangzhou, and Jinan; it was decided to hold a central meeting, which began in Shanghai on 23 July 1921. The first session of the National Congress of the Chinese Communist Party was attended by 13 delegates, Mao included. After the authorities sent a police spy to the congress, the delegates moved to a boat on South Lake near Jiaxing, in Zhejiang, to escape detection. Although Soviet and Comintern delegates attended, the first congress ignored Lenin's advice to accept a temporary alliance between the Communists and the "bourgeois democrats" who also advocated national revolution; instead they stuck to the orthodox Marxist belief that only the urban proletariat could lead a socialist revolution.

Mao was now party secretary for Hunan stationed in Changsha, and to build the party there he followed a variety of tactics. In August 1921, he founded the Self-Study University, through which readers could gain access to revolutionary literature, housed in the premises of the Society for the Study of Wang Fuzhi, a Qing dynasty Hunanese philosopher who had resisted the Manchus. He joined the YMCA Mass Education Movement to fight illiteracy, though he edited the textbooks to include radical sentiments. He continued organising workers to strike against the administration of Hunan Governor Zhao Hengti. Yet labour issues remained central. The successful and famous Anyuan coal mines strikes [zh] (contrary to later Party historians) depended on both "proletarian" and "bourgeois" strategies. Liu Shaoqi and Li Lisan and Mao not only mobilised the miners, but formed schools and cooperatives and engaged local intellectuals, gentry, military officers, merchants, Red Gang dragon heads and even church clergy. Mao's labour organizing work in the Anyuan mines also involved his wife Yang Kaihui, who worked for women's rights, including literacy and educational issues, in the nearby peasant communities. Although Mao and Yang were not the originators of this political organizing method of combining labor organizing among male workers with a focus on women's rights issues in their communities, they were among the most effective at using this method. Mao's political organizing success in the Anyuan mines resulted in Chen Duxiu inviting him to become a member of the Communist Party's Central Committee.

Mao claimed that he missed the July 1922 Second Congress of the Communist Party in Shanghai because he lost the address. Adopting Lenin's advice, the delegates agreed to an alliance with the "bourgeois democrats" of the KMT for the good of the "national revolution". Communist Party members joined the KMT, hoping to push its politics leftward. Mao enthusiastically agreed with this decision, arguing for an alliance across China's socio-economic classes, and eventually rose to become propaganda chief of the KMT. Mao was a vocal anti-imperialist and in his writings he lambasted the governments of Japan, the UK and US, describing the latter as "the most murderous of hangmen".

On the 14th of October 1934, the Red Army broke through the KMT line on the Jiangxi Soviet's south-west corner at Xinfeng with 85,000 soldiers and 15,000 party cadres and embarked on the "Long March". In order to make the escape, many of the wounded and the ill, as well as women and children, were left behind, defended by a group of guerrilla fighters whom the KMT massacred. The 100,000 who escaped headed to southern Hunan, first crossing the Xiang River after heavy fighting, and then the Wu River, in Guizhou where they took Zunyi in January 1935. Temporarily resting in the city, they held a conference; here, Mao was elected to a position of leadership, becoming Chairman of the Politburo, and de facto leader of both Party and Red Army, in part because his candidacy was supported by Soviet Premier Joseph Stalin. Insisting that they operate as a guerrilla force, he laid out a destination: the Shenshi Soviet in Shaanxi, Northern China, from where the Communists could focus on fighting the Japanese. Mao believed that in focusing on the anti- imperialist struggle, the Communists would earn the trust of the Chinese people, who in turn would renounce the KMT.

From Zunyi, Mao led his troops to Loushan Pass,

where they faced armed opposition but successfully crossed the river. Chiang flew into the area to lead his armies against Mao, but the Communists outmanoeuvred him and crossed the Jinsha River. Faced with the more difficult task of crossing the Tatu River, they managed it by fighting a battle over the Luding Bridge in May, taking Luding. Marching through the mountain ranges around Ma'anshan, in Moukung, Western Sichuan, they encountered the 50,000-strong CCP Fourth Front Army of Zhang Guotao, and together proceeded to Maoerhkai and then Gansu. Zhang and Mao disagreed over what to do; the latter wished to proceed to Shaanxi, while Zhang wanted to retreat east to Tibet or Sikkim, far from the KMT threat. It was agreed that they would go their separate ways, with Zhu De joining Zhang. Mao's forces proceeded north, through hundreds of kilometres of Grasslands, an area of quagmire where they were attacked by Manchu tribesman and where many soldiers succumbed to famine and disease. Finally reaching Shaanxi, they fought off both the KMT and an Islamic cavalry militia before crossing the Min Mountains and Mount Liupan and reaching the Shenshi Soviet; only 7,000– 8000 had survived. The Long March cemented Mao's status as the dominant figure in the party. In November 1935, he was named chairman of the Military Commission. From this point onward, Mao was the Communist Party's undisputed leader, even though he would not become party chairman until 1943.

Mao proclaimed the establishment of the People's Republic of China from the Gate of Heavenly Peace (Tian'anmen) on 1 October 1949, and later that week declared "The Chinese people have stood up" . Mao went to Moscow for long talks in the winter of 1949–50. Mao initiated the talks which focused on the political and economic revolution in China, foreign policy, railways, naval bases, and Soviet economic and technical aid. The resulting treaty reflected Stalin's dominance and his willingness to help Mao.

Mao's views as a Marxist were strongly influenced by Lenin, particularly with regard to the vanguardism. Mao believed that only the correct leadership of the Communist Party could advance China into socialism. Conversely, Mao also believed that mass movements and mass criticism were necessary in order to check the bureaucracy.

Mao pushed the Party to organise campaigns to reform society and extend control. These campaigns were given urgency in October 1950, when Mao made the decision to send the People's Volunteer Army, a special unit of the People's Liberation Army, into the Korean War and fight as well as to reinforce the armed forces of North Korea, the Korean People's Army, which had been in full retreat. The United States placed a trade embargo on the People's Republic as a result of its involvement in the Korean War, lasting until Richard Nixon's improvements of relations. At least 180 thousand Chinese troops died during the war.

Mao directed operations to the minutest detail. As the Chairman of the Central Military Commission (CMC), he was also the Supreme Commander in Chief of the PLA and the People's Republic and Chairman of the Party. Chinese troops in Korea were under the overall command of then newly installed Premier Zhou Enlai, with General Peng Dehuai as field commander and political commissar.

During the land reform campaigns, large numbers of landlords and rich peasants were beaten to death at mass meetings organised by the Communist Party as land was taken from them and given to poorer peasants, which significantly reduced economic inequality. The Campaign to Suppress Counter- revolutionaries targeted bureaucratic burgeoisie, such as compradores, merchants and Kuomintang officials who were seen by the party as economic parasites or political enemies. In 1976, the U.S. State department estimated as many as a million were killed in the land reform, and 800,000 killed in the counter- revolutionary campaign.

Mao himself claimed that a total of 700,000 people were killed in attacks on "counter-revolutionaries" during the years 1950– 1952. Because there was a policy to select "at least one landlord, and usually several, in virtually every village for public execution", the number of deaths range between 2 million and 5 million. In addition, at least 1.5 million people, perhaps as many as four to six million, were sent to "reform through labour" camps where many perished. Mao played a personal role in organising the mass repressions and established a system of execution quotas, which were often exceeded. He defended these killings as necessary for the securing of power.

The Mao government is credited with eradicating both consumption and production of opium during the 1950s using unrestrained repression and social reform. Ten million addicts were forced into compulsory treatment, dealers were executed, and opium-producing regions were planted with new crops. Remaining opium production shifted south of the Chinese border into the Golden Triangle region.

Starting in 1951, Mao initiated two successive movements in an effort to rid urban areas of corruption by targeting wealthy capitalists and political opponents, known as the three-anti/five- anti campaigns. Whereas the three-anti campaign was a focused purge of government, industrial and party officials, the five-anti campaign set its sights slightly broader, targeting capitalist elements in general. Workers denounced their bosses, spouses turned on their spouses, and children informed on their parents; the victims were often humiliated at struggle sessions, where a targeted person would be verbally and physically abused until they confessed to crimes. Mao insisted that minor offenders be criticised and reformed or sent to labour camps, "while the worst among them should be shot". These campaigns took several hundred thousand additional lives, the vast majority via suicide. In Shanghai, suicide by jumping from tall buildings became so commonplace that residents avoided walking on the pavement near skyscrapers for fear that suicides might land on them. Some biographers have pointed out that driving those perceived as enemies to suicide was a common tactic during the Mao-era. In his biography of Mao, Philip Short notes that Mao gave explicit instructions in the Yan'an Rectification Movement that "no cadre is to be killed" but in practice allowed security chief Kang Sheng to drive opponents to suicide and that "this pattern was repeated throughout his leadership of the People's Republic".

Following the consolidation of power, Mao launched the First Five-Year Plan (1953–1958), which emphasised rapid industrial development. Within industry, iron and steel, electric power, coal, heavy engineering, building materials, and basic chemicals were prioritised with the aim of constructing large and highly capital-intensive plants. Many of these plants were built with Soviet assistance and heavy industry grew rapidly. Agriculture, industry and trade was organised on a collective basis (socialist cooperatives). This period marked the beginning of China's rapid industrialisation and it resulted in an enormous success.

Despite being initially sympathetic towards the reformist government of Imre Nagy, Mao feared the "reactionary restoration" in Hungary as the Hungarian crisis continued and became more hardline. Mao opposed the withdrawal of Soviet troops by asking Liu Shaoqi to inform the Soviet representatives to maintain a hardline stance against "western imperialist- backed" protestors and Nagy's government. However, it was unclear if Mao's stance played a crucial role, if any role, in Khrushchev's decision to invade Hungary. It was also unclear if China was forced to conform to the Soviet position due to economic concerns and China's poor power projections compared to the USSR. Despite his disagreements with Moscow's hegemony in the Socialist Camp, Mao viewed the integrity of the international communist movement as more important than the national autonomy of the countries in the Soviet sphere of influence. The Hungarian Revolution also influenced Mao's Hundred Flowers Campaign. Mao decided to soften his stance on Chinese intelligentsia and allow them to express their social dissatisfaction and criticisms of the errors of the government. Mao wanted to use this movement to prevent a similar uprising in China. Programs pursued during this time include the Hundred Flowers Campaign, in which Mao indicated his supposed willingness to consider different opinions about how China should be governed. Given the freedom to express themselves, liberal and intellectual Chinese began opposing the Communist Party and questioning its leadership. This was initially tolerated and encouraged. After a few months, Mao's government reversed its policy and persecuted those who had criticised the party, totalling perhaps 500,000, as well as those who were merely alleged to have been critical, in what is called the Anti-Rightist Movement.

Li Zhisui, Mao's physician, suggested that Mao had initially seen the policy as a way of weakening opposition to him within the party and that he was surprised by the extent of criticism and the fact that it came to be directed at his own leadership.

In January 1958, Mao launched the second Five-Year Plan, known as the Great Leap Forward, a plan intended to turn China from an agrarian nation to an industrialised one and as an alternative model for economic growth to the Soviet model focusing on heavy industry that was advocated by others in the party. Under this economic program, the relatively small agricultural collectives that had been formed to date were rapidly merged into far larger people's communes, and many of the peasants were ordered to work on massive infrastructure projects and on the production of iron and steel. Some private food production was banned, and livestock and farm implements were brought under collective ownership.

Under the Great Leap Forward, Mao and other party leaders ordered the implementation of a variety of unproven and unscientific new agricultural techniques by the new communes. The combined effect of the diversion of labour to steel production and infrastructure projects, and cyclical natural disasters led to an approximately 15% drop in grain production in 1959 followed by a further 10% decline in 1960 and no recovery in 1961.

In an effort to win favour with their superiors and avoid being purged, each layer in the party exaggerated the amount of grain produced under them. Based upon the falsely reported success, party cadres were ordered to requisition a disproportionately high amount of that fictitious harvest for state use, primarily for use in the cities and urban areas but also for export. The result, compounded in some areas by drought and in others by floods, was that farmers were left with little food for themselves and many millions starved to death in the Great Chinese Famine. The people of urban areas in China were given food stamps each month, but the people of rural areas were expected to grow their own crops and give some of the crops back to the government. The death count in rural parts of China surpassed the deaths in the urban centres. Additionally, the Chinese government continued to export food that could have been allocated to the country's starving citizens. The famine was a direct cause of the death of some 30 million Chinese peasants between 1959 and 1962. Furthermore, many children who became malnourished during years of hardship died after the Great Leap Forward came to an end in 1962.

In late autumn 1958, Mao condemned the practices that were being used during Great Leap Forward such as forcing peasants to do exhausting labour without enough food or rest which resulted in epidemics and starvation. He also acknowledged that anti-rightist campaigns were a major cause of "production at the expense of livelihood." He refused to abandon the Great Leap Forward to solve these difficulties, but he did demand that they be confronted. After the July 1959 clash at Lushan Conference with Peng Dehuai, Mao launched a new anti-rightist campaign along with the radical policies that he previously abandoned. It wasn't until the spring of 1960, that Mao would again express concern about abnormal deaths and other abuses, but he did not move to stop them. Bernstein concludes that the Chairman "wilfully ignored the lessons of the first radical phase for the sake of achieving extreme ideological and developmental goals". Some writers note that Mao was dismissive of reports he received of food shortages in the countryside and refused to change course, believing that peasants were lying and that rightists and kulaks were hoarding grain. He refused to open state granaries, and instead launched a series of "anti-grain concealment" drives that resulted in numerous purges and suicides. Other violent campaigns followed in which party leaders went from village to village in search of hidden food reserves, and not only grain, as Mao issued quotas for pigs, chickens, ducks and eggs. Many peasants accused of hiding food were tortured and beaten to death.

The extent of Mao's knowledge of the severity of the situation has been disputed. Mao's personal physician, Li Zhisui, said that Mao may have been unaware of the extent of the famine, partly due to a reluctance of local officials to criticise his policies, and the willingness of his staff to exaggerate or outright fake reports. Li writes that upon learning of the extent of the starvation, Mao vowed to stop eating meat, an action followed by his staff. Mao stepped down as President of China on the 27th of April 1959; however, he retained other top positions such as Chairman of the Communist Party and of the Central Military Commission. The Presidency was transferred to Liu Shaoqi. He was eventually forced to abandon the policy in 1962, and he lost political power to Liu Shaoqi and Deng Xiaoping.

The Great Leap Forward was a tragedy for the vast majority of the Chinese. Although the steel quotas were officially reached, almost all of the supposed steel made in the countryside was iron, as it had been made from assorted scrap metal in home-made furnaces with no reliable source of fuel such as coal. This meant that proper smelting conditions could not be achieved. According to Zhang Rongmei, a geometry teacher in rural Shanghai during the Great Leap Forward: "We took all the furniture, pots, and pans we had in our house, and all our neighbours did likewise. We put everything in a big fire and melted down all the metal". The worst of the famine was steered towards enemies of the state. The most vulnerable section of China's population, around five percent, were those whom Mao called 'enemies of the people'. Anyone who had in previous campaigns of repression been labeled a 'black element' was given the lowest priority in the allocation of food. Landlords, rich peasants, former members of the nationalist regime, religious leaders, rightists, counter-revolutionaries and the families of such individuals died in the greatest numbers."

According to official Chinese statistics for Second Five-Year Plan (1958–1962):"industrial output value value had doubled; the gross value of agricultural products increased by 35 percent; steel production in 1962 was between 10.6 million tons or 12 million tons; investment in capital construction rose to 40 percent from 35 percent in the First Five-Year Plan period; the investment in capital construction was doubled; and the average income of workers and farmers increased by up to 30 percent." At a large Communist Party conference in Beijing in January 1962, dubbed the "Seven Thousand Cadres Conference", State Chairman Liu Shaoqi denounced the Great Leap Forward, attributing the project to widespread famine in China. The overwhelming majority of delegates expressed agreement, but Defense Minister Lin Biao staunchly defended Mao. A brief period of liberalisation followed while Mao and Lin plotted a comeback. Liu Shaoqi and Deng Xiaoping rescued the economy by disbanding the people's communes, introducing elements of private control of peasant smallholdings and importing grain from Canada and Australia to mitigate the worst effects of famine.

At the Lushan Conference in July/August 1959, several ministers expressed concern that the Great Leap Forward had not proved as successful as planned. The most direct of these was Minister of Defence and Korean War veteran General Peng Dehuai. Following Peng's criticism of the Great Leap Forward, Mao orchestrated a purge of Peng and his supporters, stifling criticism of the Great Leap policies.

Senior officials who reported the truth of the famine to Mao were branded as "right opportunists." A campaign against right-wing opportunism was launched and resulted in party members and ordinary peasants being sent to prison labour camps where many would subsequently die in the famine. Years later the CCP would conclude that as many as six million people were wrongly punished in the campaign.

The number of deaths by starvation during the Great Leap Forward is deeply controversial. Until the mid-1980s, when official census figures were finally published by the Chinese Government, little was known about the scale of the disaster in the Chinese countryside, as the handful of Western observers allowed access during this time had been restricted to model villages where they were deceived into believing that the Great Leap Forward had been a great success. There was also an assumption that the flow of individual reports of starvation that had been reaching the West, primarily through Hong Kong and Taiwan, must have been localised or exaggerated as China was continuing to claim record harvests and was a net exporter of grain through the period. Because Mao wanted to pay back early to the Soviets debts totalling 1.973 billion yuan from 1960 to 1962, exports increased by 50%, and fellow Communist regimes in North Korea, North Vietnam and Albania were provided grain free of charge.

Censuses were carried out in China in 1953, 1964 and 1982. The first attempt to analyse this data to estimate the number of famine deaths was carried out by American demographer Dr. Judith Banister and published in 1984. Given the lengthy gaps between the censuses and doubts over the reliability of the data, an accurate figure is difficult to ascertain. Nevertheless, Banister concluded that the official data implied that around 15 million excess deaths incurred in China during 1958–61, and that based on her modelling of Chinese demographics during the period and taking account of assumed under-reporting during the famine years, the figure was around thirty million.

A high-ranking official of the CCP, stated that twenty million people died according to official government statistics. Yang Jisheng, a former Xinhua News Agency reporter who had privileged access and connections available to no other scholars, estimates a death toll of 36 million. Frank Dikötter estimates that there were at least forty-five million premature deaths attributable to the Great Leap Forward from 1958 to 1962. Various other sources have put the figure at between twenty and forty-six million.

During the early 1960s, Mao became concerned with the nature of post-1959 China. He saw that the revolution and Great Leap Forward had replaced the old ruling elite with a new one. He was concerned that those in power were becoming estranged from the people they were to serve. Mao believed that a revolution of culture would unseat and unsettle the "ruling class" and keep China in a state of "continuous revolution" that, theoretically, would serve the interests of the majority, rather than a tiny and privileged elite. State Chairman Liu Shaoqi and General Secretary Deng Xiaoping favoured the idea that Mao be removed from actual power as China's head of state and government but maintain his ceremonial and symbolic role as Chairman of the Chinese Communist Party, with the party upholding all of his positive contributions to the revolution. They attempted to marginalise Mao by taking control of economic policy and asserting themselves politically as well. Many claim that Mao responded to Liu and Deng's movements by launching the Great Proletarian Cultural Revolution in 1966. Some scholars, such as Mobo Gao, claim the case for this is overstated. Others, such as

Frank Dikötter, hold that Mao launched the Cultural Revolution to wreak revenge on those who had dared to challenge him over the Great Leap Forward.

The Cultural Revolution led to the destruction of much of China's traditional cultural heritage and the imprisonment of a huge number of Chinese citizens, as well as the creation of general economic and social chaos in the country. Millions of lives were ruined during this period, as the Cultural Revolution pierced into every part of Chinese life, depicted by such Chinese films as To Live, The Blue Kite and Farewell My Concubine. It is estimated that hundreds of thousands of people, perhaps millions, perished in the violence of the Cultural Revolution. This included prominent figures such as Liu Shaoqi.

When Mao was informed of such losses, particularly that people had been driven to suicide, he is alleged to have commented: "People who try to commit suicide—don't attempt to save them! ... China is such a populous nation, it is not as if we cannot do without a few people." The authorities allowed the Red Guards to abuse and kill opponents of the regime. Said Xie Fuzhi, national police chief: "Don't say it is wrong of them to beat up bad persons: if in anger they beat someone to death, then so be it." In August and September 1966, there were a reported 1,772 people murdered by the Red Guards in Beijing alone.

It was during this period that Mao chose Lin Biao, who seemed to echo all of Mao's ideas, to become his successor. Lin was later officially named as Mao's successor. By 1971, a divide between the two men had become apparent. Official history in China states that Lin was planning a military coup or an assassination attempt on Mao. Lin Biao died on 13 September 1971, in a plane crash over the air space of Mongolia, presumably as he fled China, probably anticipating his arrest. The CCP declared that Lin was planning to depose Mao and posthumously expelled Lin from the party. At this time, Mao lost trust in many of the top CCP figures. The highest-ranking Soviet Bloc intelligence defector, Lt. Gen. Ion Mihai Pacepa claimed he had a conversation with Nicolae Ceauşescu, who told him about a plot to kill Mao Zedong with the help of Lin Biao organised by the KGB.

Despite being considered a feminist figure by some and a supporter of women's rights, documents released by the US Department of State in 2008 show that Mao declared women to be a "nonsense" in 1973, in conversation with Henry Kissinger, joking that "China is a very poor country. We don't have much. What we have in excess is women. Let them go to your place. They will create disasters. That way you can lessen our burdens." When Mao offered 10 million women, Kissinger replied by saying that Mao was "improving his offer". Mao and Kissinger then agreed that their comments on women be removed from public records, prompted by a Chinese official who feared that Mao's comments might incur public anger if released.

In 1969, Mao declared the Cultural Revolution to be over, although various historians in and outside of China mark the end of the Cultural Revolution—as a whole or in part—in 1976, following Mao's death and the arrest of the Gang of Four. The Central Committee in 1981 officially declared the Cultural Revolution a "severe setback" for the PRC. It is often looked at in all scholarly circles as a greatly disruptive period for China. Despite the pro-poor rhetoric of Mao's regime, his economic policies led to substantial poverty.

Estimates of the death toll during the Cultural Revolution, including civilians and Red Guards, vary greatly. An estimate of around 400,000 deaths is a widely accepted minimum figure, according to Maurice Meisner. MacFarquhar and Schoenhals assert that in rural China alone some 36 million people were persecuted, of whom between 750,000 and 1.5 million were killed, with roughly the same number permanently injured. Mao's health declined in his last years, probably aggravated by his chain-smoking. It became a state secret that he suffered from multiple lung and heart ailments during his later years. There are unconfirmed reports that he possibly had Parkinson's disease in addition to amyotrophic lateral sclerosis, also known as Lou Gehrig's disease. His final public appearance—and the last known photograph of him alive—had been on the 27th of May 1976, when he met the visiting Pakistani Prime Minister Zulfikar Ali Bhutto. He suffered two major heart attacks, one in March and another in July, then a third on the 5th of September, rendering him an invalid. He died nearly four days later, at 00:10 on the 9th of September 1976, at the age of eighty-two. The Communist Party delayed the announcement of his death until 4pm, when a national radio broadcast announced the news and appealed for party unity.

Mao's embalmed body, draped in the CCP flag, lay in state at the Great Hall of the People for one week. One million Chinese filed past to pay their final respects, many crying openly or displaying sadness, while foreigners watched on television. Mao's official portrait hung on the wall with a banner reading: "Carry on the cause left by Chairman Mao and carry on the cause of proletarian revolution to the end". On 17 September the body was taken in a minibus to the 305 Hospital, where his internal organs were preserved in formaldehyde.

On the 18th of September, guns, sirens, whistles and horns across China were simultaneously blown and a mandatory three- minute silence was observed. Tiananmen Square was packed with millions of people and a military band played "The Internationale". Hua Guofeng concluded the service with a twenty minute-long eulogy atop Tiananmen Gate. Despite Mao's request to be cremated, his body was later permanently put on display in the Mausoleum of Mao Zedong, in order for the Chinese nation to pay it's respects.

Francisco Franco

Francisco Franco was a Spanish military general who led the Nationalist forces in overthrowing the Second Spanish Republic during the Spanish Civil War and thereafter ruled over Spain from 1939 to 1975 as a dictator, assuming the title Caudillo. This period in Spanish history, from the Nationalist victory to Franco's death, is commonly known as Francoist Spain or as the Francoist dictatorship.

Born in Ferrol, Galicia, into an upper-class military family, Franco served in the Spanish Army as a cadet in the Toledo Infantry Academy from 1907 to 1910. While serving in Morocco, he rose through the ranks to become a brigadier general in 1926 at age thirty-three, which made him the youngest general in all of Europe. Two years later, Franco became the director of the General Military Academy in Zaragoza. As a conservative and monarchist, Franco regretted the abolition of the monarchy and the establishment of the Second Republic in 1931, and was devastated by the closing of his academy; nevertheless, he continued his service in the Republican Army. His career was boosted after the right-wing CEDA and PRR won the 1933 election, empowering him to lead the suppression of the 1934 uprising in Asturias. Franco was briefly elevated to Chief of Army Staff before the 1936 election moved the leftist Popular Front into power, relegating him to the Canary Islands. Initially reluctant, he joined the July 1936 military coup, which, after failing to take Spain, sparked the Spanish Civil War.

During the war, he commanded Spain's African colonial army and later, following the deaths of much of the rebel leadership, became his faction's only leader, being appointed Generalissimo and head of state in 1936. He consolidated all nationalist parties into the FET y de las JONS (creating a one-party state) and developed a cult of personality around his rule by founding the Movimiento Nacional. Three years later the Nationalists declared victory, which extended Franco's dictatorship over Spain through a period of repression of political opponents. His dictatorship's use of forced labor, concentration camps and executions led to between 30,000 and 50,000 deaths. Combined with wartime killings, this brings the death toll of the White Terror to between 100,000 and 200,000.

During World War II Franco maintained Spanish neutrality, but supported the Axis—whose members Italy and Germany had supported him during the Civil War—damaging the country's international reputation in various ways. During the start of the Cold War, Franco lifted Spain out of its mid-20th century economic depression through technocratic and economically liberal policies, presiding over a period of accelerated growth known as the "Spanish miracle". At the same time, his regime transitioned from a totalitarian state to an authoritarian one with limited pluralism. He became a leader in the anti- Communist movement, garnering support from the West, particularly the United States. As the dictatorship relaxed its hard-line policies, Luis Carrero Blanco became Franco's éminence grise, whose role expanded after Franco began struggling with Parkinson's disease in the 1960s. In 1973, Franco resigned as prime minister—separated from the office of head of state since 1967—due to his advanced age and illness. Nevertheless, he remained in power as the head of state and as commander-in-chief. Franco died in 1975, aged eighty-two, and was entombed in the Valle de los Caídos. He restored the monarchy in his final years, being succeeded by Juan Carlos, King of Spain, who led the Spanish transition to democracy.

The legacy of Franco in Spanish history remains controversial, as the nature of his dictatorship changed over time. His reign was marked by both brutal repression, with tens of thousands killed, and economic prosperity, which greatly improved the quality of life in Spain. His dictatorial style proved adaptable enough to allow social and economic reform, but still centred on highly centralised government, authoritarianism, nationalism, national Catholicism, anti-freemasonry and anti-Communism.

Francisco Franco was born on the 4th of December 1892 in the Calle Frutos Saavedra in El Ferrol, Galicia, into a seafaring family. After relocating to Galicia, the Franco family was involved in the Spanish Navy, and over the span of two centuries produced naval officers for six uninterrupted generations (including several admirals), down to Franco's father, Nicolás Franco Salgado-Araújo. His mother, María , was from an upper- middle-class Roman Catholic family. The young Franco spent much of his childhood with his two brothers, Nicolás and Ramón, and his two sisters, María del Pilar and María de la Paz. Franco's father was a naval officer who reached the rank of vice admiral (intendente general). When Franco was fourteen, his father moved to Madrid following a reassignment and ultimately abandoned his family, marrying another woman. While Franco did not suffer any great abuse by his father's hand, he would never overcome his antipathy for his father and largely ignored him for the rest of his life. Years after becoming dictator, under the pseudonym Jaime de Andrade, Franco wrote a brief novel called Raza, whose protagonist is believed by Stanley Payne to represent the idealised man Franco wished his father had been. Conversely, Franco strongly identified with his mother and learned from her moderation, austerity, self-control, family solidarity and respect for Catholicism, though he would also inherit his father's harshness, coldness and implacability.

Francisco followed his father into the Navy, but as a result of the Spanish American War the country lost much of its navy as well as most of its colonies. Not needing any more officers, the Naval Academy admitted no new entrants from 1906 to 1913. To his father's chagrin, Francisco decided to try the Spanish Army. In 1907, he entered the Infantry Academy in Toledo. At the age of fourteen, Franco was one of the youngest members of his class, with most boys being between sixteen and eighteen. He was short and was bullied for his small size. His grades were average; though his good memory meant he seldom struggled academically, his small stature was a hindrance in physical tests. He graduated in July 1910 as a second lieutenant, standing 251st out of 312 cadets in his class, though this might have had less to do with his grades than with his small size and young age. Franco was promoted to the rank of first lieutenant in June 1912 at age nineteen. Two years later, he obtained a commission to Morocco. Spanish efforts to occupy the new African protectorate provoked the Second Melillan campaign in 1909 against native Moroccans, the first of several Riffian rebellions. Their tactics resulted in heavy losses among Spanish military officers, and also provided an opportunity to earn promo-

tion through merit on the battlefield. It was said that officers would receive either la caja o la faja (a coffin or a general's sash). Franco quickly gained a reputation as an
effective officer.

In 1913, Franco transferred into the newly formed regulares: Moroccan colonial troops with Spanish officers,
who acted as elite shock troops. In 1916, aged 23 with the
rank of captain, Franco was shot in the abdomen by
guerilla gunfire during an assault on Moroccan positions
at El Biutz, in the hills near Ceuta; this was the only time
he was wounded in ten years of fighting. The wound was
serious, and he was not expected to live. His recovery was
seen by his Moroccan troops as a spiritual event – they
believed Franco to be blessed with baraka, or protected by
God. He was recommended for promotion to major and to
receive Spain's highest honour for gallantry, the coveted
Cruz Laureada de San Fernando. Both proposals were
denied, with the 23-year-old Franco's young age being
given as the reason for denial. Franco appealed the decision to the king, who reversed it. Franco also received the
Cross of Maria Cristina, First Class.

With that he was promoted to major at the end of February 1917 at age twenty-four. This made him the youngest
major in the Spanish army. From 1917 to 1920, he served
in Spain. In 1920, Lieutenant Colonel José Millán
Astray, a histrionic but charismatic officer, founded the
Spanish Foreign Legion, along similar lines as the French
Foreign Legion. Franco became the Legion's second-in-
command and returned to Africa. In the Rif War, the
poorly commanded and overextended Spanish Army was
defeated by the Republic of the Rif under the leadership of
the Abd el-Krim brothers, who crushed a Spanish offensive on the 24th of July 1921, at Annual. The Legion and
supporting units relieved the Spanish city of Melilla

after a three-day forced march led by Franco. In 1923, now a lieutenant colonel, he was made commander of the Legion.

On the 22nd of October 1923, Franco married María del Carmen Polo y Martínez-Valdès. Following his honeymoon Franco was summoned to Madrid to be presented to King Alfonso XIII. This and other occasions of royal attention would mark him during the Republic as a monarchical officer.

Disappointed with the plans for a strategic retreat from the interior to the African coastline by Primo de Rivera, Franco wrote in the April 1924 issue of Revista de Tropas Coloniales (Colonial Troops Magazine) that he would disobey orders of retreat given by a superior. He also held a tense meeting with Primo de Rivera in July 1924. According to fellow africanista, Gonzalo Queipo de Llano, Franco visited him on the 21st of September 1924 to propose that he lead a coup d'état against Primo. In the end, Franco complied with Primo's orders, taking part in the retreat of Spanish soldiers from Xaouen [es] in late 1924, and thus earning a promotion to colonel.

Franco led the first wave of troops ashore at Al Hoceima (Spanish: Alhucemas) in 1925. This landing in the heartland of Abd el-Krim's tribe, combined with the French invasion from the south, spelled the beginning of the end for the short-lived Republic of the Rif. Franco was eventually recognised for his leadership, and he was promoted to brigadier general.

On the 14th of September 1926, Franco and Polo had a daughter, María del Carmen. Franco would have a close relationship with his daughter and was a proud parent, though his traditionalist attitudes and increasing responsibilities meant he left much of the child-rearing to his wife. In 1928 Franco was appointed director of the newly created General Military Academy of Zaragoza, a new college for all Spanish army cadets, replacing the former separate institutions for young men seeking to become officers in infantry, cavalry, artillery, and other branches of the army. Franco was removed as Director of the Zaragoza Military Academy in 1931; when the Civil War began, the colonels, majors, and captains of the Spanish Army who had attended the academy when he was its director displayed unconditional loyalty to him as Caudillo.

The municipal elections of the 12th of April 1931 were largely seen as a plebiscite on the monarchy. The Republican-Socialist alliance failed to win the majority of the municipalities in Spain, but had a landslide victory in all the large cities and in almost all the provincial capitals. The monarchists and the army deserted Alfonso XIII and consequently the king decided to leave the country and go into exile, giving way to the Second Spanish Republic. Although Franco believed that the majority of the Spanish people still supported the crown, and although he regretted the end of the monarchy, he did not object, nor did he challenge the legitimacy of the republic. The closing of the academy in June by the provisional War Minister Manuel Azaña however was a major setback for Franco and provoked his first clash with the Spanish Republic. Azaña found Franco's farewell speech to the cadets insulting. In his speech Franco stressed the Republic's need for discipline and respect. Azaña entered an official reprimand into Franco's personnel file and for six months Franco was without a post and under surveillance.

In December 1931, a new reformist, liberal, and democratic constitution was declared. It included strong provisions enforcing a broad secularisation of the Catholic country, which included the abolishing of Catholic schools and charities, which many moderate committed Catholics opposed. At this point, once the constituent assembly had fulfilled its mandate of approving a new constitution, it should have arranged for regular parliamentary elections and adjourned, according to historian Carlton J. H. Hayes. Fearing the increasing popular opposition, the Radical and Socialist majority postponed the regular elections, thereby prolonging their stay in power for two more years. This way the republican government of Manuel Azaña initiated numerous reforms to what in their view would "modernize" the country.

Franco was a subscriber to the journal of Acción Española, a monarchist organisation, and a firm believer in a supposed Jewish-Masonic-Bolshevik conspiracy, or contubernio (conspiracy). The conspiracy suggested that Jews, Freemasons, Communists, and other leftists alike sought the destruction of Christian Europe, with Spain being the principal target.

On the 5th of February 1932, Franco was given a command in A Coruña. Franco avoided involvement in José Sanjurjo's attempted coup that year, and even wrote a hostile letter to Sanjurjo expressing his anger over the attempt. As a result of Azaña's military reform, in January 1933 Franco was relegated from first to 24th in the list of brigadiers. The same year, on the 17th of February he was given the military command of the Balearic Islands. The post was above his rank, but Franco was still unhappy that he was stuck in a position he disliked. The prime minister wrote in his diary that it was probably more prudent to have Franco away from Madrid.

In 1932, the Jesuits, who were in charge of many schools throughout the country, were banned and had all their property confiscated. The army was further reduced and landowners were expropriated. Home rule was granted to Catalonia, with a local parliament and a president of its own. In June 1933 Pope Pius XI issued the encyclical Dilectissima Nobis (Our Dearly Beloved), "On Oppression of the Church of Spain", in which he criticised the anti-clericalism of the Republican government.

The elections held in October 1933 resulted in a centre-right majority. The political party with the most votes was the Confederación Español de Derechas Autónomas ("CEDA"), but president Alcalá-Zamora declined to invite the leader of the CEDA, Gil Robles, to form a government. Instead he invited the Radical Republican Party's Alejandro Lerroux to do so. Despite receiving the most votes, CEDA was denied cabinet positions for nearly a year. After a year of intense pressure, CEDA, the largest party in the congress, was finally successful in forcing the acceptance of three ministries. The entrance of CEDA in the government, despite being normal in a parliamentary democracy, was not well accepted by the left. The Socialists triggered an insurrection that they had been preparing for nine months. The leftist Republican parties did not directly join the insurrection, but their leadership issued statements that they were "breaking all relations" with the Republican government. The Catalan Bloc Obrer i Camperol (BOC) advocated the need to form a broad workers' front, and took the lead in forming a new and more encompassing Alianza Obrera, which included the Catalan UGT and the Catalan sector of the PSOE, with the goal of defeating fascism and advancing the socialist revolution. The Alianza Obrera declared a general strike "against fascism" in Catalonia in 1934. A Catalan state was proclaimed by Catalan nationalist leader Lluis Companys, but it lasted just ten hours. Despite an attempt at a general stoppage in Madrid, other strikes did not endure. This left the striking Asturian miners to fight alone.

In several mining towns in Asturias, local unions gathered small arms and were determined to see the strike through. It began on the evening of the 4th of October, with the miners occupying several towns, attacking and seizing local Civil and Assault Guard barracks. Thirty four priests, six young seminarists with ages between 18 and 21, and several businessmen and civil guards were summarily executed by the revolutionaries in Mieres and Sama, 58 religious buildings including churches, convents and part of the university at Oviedo were burned and destroyed, and over 100 priests were killed in the diocese. Franco, already General of Division and aide to the war minister, Diego Hidalgo, was put in command of the operations directed to suppress the violent insurgency. Troops of the Spanish Army of Africa carried this out, with General Eduardo López Ochoa as commander in the field. After two weeks of heavy fighting (and a death toll estimated between 1,200 and 2,000), the rebellion was suppressed.

The insurgency in Asturias in October 1934 sparked a new era of violent anti-Christian persecutions with the massacre of thirty- four priests, initiating the practice of atrocities against the clergy, and sharpened the antagonism between Left and Right. Franco and López Ochoa (who, prior to the campaign in Asturias, had been seen as a left-leaning officer) emerged as officers prepared to use "troops against Spanish civilians as if they were a foreign enemy". Franco described the rebellion to a journalist in Oviedo as, "a frontier war and its fronts are socialism, communism and whatever attacks civilisation to replace it with barbarism." Though the colonial units sent to the north by the government at Franco's recommendation consisted of the Spanish Foreign Legion and the Moroccan Regulares Indigenas, the right-wing press portrayed the Asturian rebels as lackeys of a foreign Jewish-Bolshevik conspiracy.

With this rebellion against legitimate established political authority, the socialists also repudiated the representative institutional system as the anarchists had done. The Spanish historian Salvador de Madariaga, an Azaña supporter, and an exiled vocal opponent of Francisco Franco is the author of a sharp critical reflection against the participation of the left in the revolt: "The uprising of 1934 is unforgivable. The argument that Mr Gil Robles tried to destroy the Constitution to establish fascism was, at once, hypocritical and false. With the rebellion of 1934, the Spanish left lost even the shadow of moral authority to condemn the rebellion of 1936."

At the start of the Civil War, López Ochoa was assassinated; his head was severed and paraded around the streets on a pole, with a card reading, 'This is the butcher of Asturias'. Some time after these events, Franco was briefly commander-in-chief of the Army of Africa, from the 15th of February onwards, and from the 19th of May 1935 on, Chief of the General Staff.

At the end of 1935, President Alcalá-Zamora manipulated a petty-corruption issue into a major scandal in parliament, and eliminated Alejandro Lerroux, the head of the Radical Republican Party, from the premiership. Subsequently, Alcalá-Zamora vetoed the logical replacement, a majority center-right coalition, led by the CEDA, which would reflect the composition of the parliament. He then arbitrarily appointed an interim prime minister and after a short period announced the dissolution of parliament and new elections.

Two wide coalitions formed: the Popular Front on the left, ranging from Republican Union to Communists, and the Frente Nacional on the right, ranging from the centre radicals to the conservative Carlists. On 16 February 1936 the elections ended in a virtual draw, but in the evening leftist mobs started to interfere in the balloting and in the registration of votes, distorting the results. Stanley G. Payne claims that the process was blatant electoral fraud, with widespread violation of the laws and the constitution. In line with Payne's point of view, in 2017 two Spanish scholars, Manuel Álvarez Tardío and Roberto Villa García published the result of a major research work in which they concluded that the 1936 elections were rigged, a view disputed by Paul Preston, and other scholars such as Iker Itoiz Ciáurriz, who denounces their conclusions as revisionist "classic Francoist anti-republican tropes".

On the 19th of February, the cabinet presided over by Portela Valladares resigned, with a new cabinet being quickly set up, composed chiefly of members of the Republican Left and the Republican Union and presided over by Manuel Azaña.

José Calvo Sotelo, who made anti-communism the focus of his parliamentary speeches, began spreading violent propaganda— advocating for a military coup d'état; formulating a catastrophist discourse of a dichotomous choice between "communism" or a markedly totalitarian "National" State, and setting the mood of the masses for a military rebellion. The diffusion of the myth about an alleged Communist coup d'état as well a pretended state of "social chaos" became pretexts for a coup. Franco himself along with General Emilio Mola had stirred an anti- Communist campaign in Morocco.

At the same time PSOE's left-wing socialists became more radical. Julio Álvarez del Vayo talked about "Spain's being converted into a socialist Republic in association with the Soviet Union". Francisco Largo Caballero declared that "the organized proletariat will carry everything before it and destroy everything until we reach our goal". The country rapidly descended into anarchy. Even the staunch socialist Indalecio Prieto, at a party rally in Cuenca in May 1936, complained: "We Spaniards have never seen so tragic a panorama or so great a collapse as in Spain at this moment. Abroad, Spain is classified as insolvent. This is not the road to socialism or communism but to desperate anarchism without even the advantage of liberty."

On the 23rd of February, Franco was sent to the Canary Islands to serve as the islands' military commander, an appointment perceived by him as a destierro (banishment). Meanwhile, a conspiracy led by General Mola was taking shape.

Interested in the parliamentary immunity granted by a seat at the Cortes, Franco intended to stand as candidate of the Right Bloc alongside José Antonio Primo de Rivera for the by-election in the province of Cuenca programmed for the 3rd of May 1936, after the results of the February 1936 election were annulled in the constituency. But Primo de Rivera refused to run alongside a military officer (Franco in particular) and Franco himself ultimately desisted on the 26th of April, one day before the decision of the election authority. By that time, PSOE politician Indalecio Prieto had already deemed Franco as a "possible caudillo for a military uprising".

Disenchantment with Azaña's rule continued to grow and was dramatically voiced by Miguel de Unamuno, a republican and one of Spain's most respected intellectuals, who in June 1936 told a reporter who published his statement in El Adelanto that President Manuel Azaña should "... debiera suicidarse como acto patriótico" ("commit suicide as a patriotic act").

In June 1936, Franco was contacted and a secret meeting was held within La Esperanza forest on Tenerife to discuss starting a military coup. An obelisk (which has subsequently been removed) commemorating this historic meeting was erected at the site in a clearing at Las Raíces in Tenerife.

Outwardly, Franco maintained an ambiguous attitude until nearly July. On the 23rd of June 1936, he wrote to the head of the government, Casares Quiroga, offering to quell the discontent in the Spanish Republican Army, but received no reply. The other rebels were determined to go ahead con Paquito o sin Paquito (with Paquito or without Paquito; Paquito being a diminutive of Paco, which in turn is short for Francisco), as it was put by José Sanjurjo, the honorary leader of the military uprising. After various postponements, the 18th of July was fixed as the date of the uprising. The situation reached a point of no return and, as presented to Franco by Mola, the coup was unavoidable and he had to choose a side. He decided to join the rebels and was given the task of commanding the Army of Africa. A privately owned DH 89 De Havilland Dragon Rapide, flown by two British pilots, Cecil Bebb and Hugh Pollard, was chartered in England on the 11th of July to take Franco to Africa.

The coup underway was precipitated by the assassination of the right-wing opposition leader Calvo Sotelo in retaliation for the murder of assault guard José Castillo, which had been committed by a group headed by a civil guard and composed of assault guards and members of the socialist militias. On the 17th of July, one day earlier than planned, the Army of Africa rebelled, detaining their commanders. On the 18th of July, Franco published a manifesto and left for Africa, where he arrived the next day to take command.

A week later the rebels, who soon called themselves the Nationalists, controlled a third of Spain; most naval units remained under control of the Republican loyalist forces, which left Franco isolated. The coup had failed in the attempt to bring a swift victory, but the Spanish Civil War had begun.

Franco rose to power during the Spanish Civil War, which began in July 1936 and officially ended with the victory of his Nationalist forces in April 1939. Although it is impossible to calculate precise statistics concerning the Spanish Civil War and its aftermath, Payne writes that if civilian fatalities above the norm are added to the total number of deaths for victims of violence, the number of deaths attributable to the civil war would reach approximately 344,000. During the war, rape, torture, and summary executions committed by soldiers under Franco's command were used as a means of retaliation and to repress political dissent.

The war was marked by foreign intervention on behalf of both sides. Franco's Nationalists were supported by Fascist Italy, which sent the Corpo Truppe Volontarie and by Nazi Germany, which sent the Condor Legion. Italian aircraft stationed on Majorca bombed Barcelona thirteen times, dropping forty-four tons of bombs aimed at civilians. These attacks were requested by General Franco as retribution against the Catalan population.

Similarly, both Italian and German planes bombed the Basque town of Guernica at Franco's request. The Republican opposition was supported by communists, socialists, and anarchists within Spain as well as the Soviet Union and volunteers who fought in the International Brigades.

Following the pronunciamiento of the 18th of July 1936, Franco assumed the leadership of the 30,000 soldiers of the Spanish Army of Africa. The first days of the insurgency were marked by an imperative need to secure control over the Spanish Moroccan Protectorate. On one side, Franco had to win the support of the native Moroccan population and their (nominal) authorities, and, on the other, he had to ensure his control over the army. His method was the summary execution of some 200 senior officers loyal to the Republic (one of them his own cousin). His loyal bodyguard was shot by Manuel Blanco. Franco's first problem was how to move his troops to the Iberian Peninsula, since most units of the Navy had remained in control of the Republic and were blocking the Strait of Gibraltar. He requested help from Benito Mussolini, who responded with an offer of arms and planes. In Germany Wilhelm Canaris, the head of the Abwehr military intelligence service, persuaded Hitler to support the Nationalists; Hitler sent twenty Ju 52 transport aircraft and six Heinkel biplane fighters, on the condition that they were not to be used in hostilities unless the Republicans attacked first. Mussolini sent 12 Savoia-Marchetti SM.81 transport/bombers, and a few fighter aircraft. From 20 July onward Franco was able, with this small squadron of aircraft, to initiate an air bridge that carried 1,500 soldiers of the Army of Africa to Seville, where these troops helped to ensure rebel control of the city. Through representatives, he started to negotiate with the United Kingdom, Germany, and Italy for more military support, and above all for more aircraft. Negotiations were successful with the Germany and Italy on the 25th of July and aircraft began to arrive in Tetouan on the 2nd of August. On the 5th of August Franco was able to break the blockade with the newly arrived air support, successfully deploying a convoy of fishing boats and merchant ships carrying some 3,000 soldiers.

On the 26th of July, just eight days after the revolt had started, foreign allies of the Republican government convened an international communist conference at Prague to arrange plans to help the Popular Front forces in Spain.

It decided to raise an international brigade of 5,000 men and a fund of 1 billion francs to be administered by a committee of five in which Largo Caballero and Dolores Ibárruri ("la Pasionaria") had prominent roles. At the same time communist parties throughout the world quickly launched a full scale propaganda campaign in support of the Popular Front. The Communist International (Comintern) immediately reinforced its activity, sending to Spain its Secretary-General, the Bulgarian Georgi Dimitrov, and Palmiro Togliatti the chief of the Communist Party of Italy. From August onward, aid from the Soviet Union began; by February 1937 two ships per day arrived at Spain's Mediterranean ports carrying munitions, rifles, machine guns, hand grenades, artillery, and trucks. With the cargo came Soviet agents, technicians, instructors and propagandists.

The Communist International immediately started to organize the International Brigades, volunteer military units which included the Garibaldi Brigade from Italy and the Lincoln Battalion from the United States. The International Brigades were usually deployed as shock troops, and as a result they suffered high casualties. In early August, the situation in western Andalucia was stable enough to allow Franco to organise a column (some 15,000 men at its height), under the command of then Lieutenant-Colonel Juan Yagüe, which would march through Extremadura towards Madrid. On the 11th of August Mérida was taken, and on the 15th of August Badajoz, thus joining both nationalist-controlled areas. Additionally, Mussolini ordered a voluntary army, the Corpo Truppe Volontarie (CTV) of fully motorised units (some 12,000 Italians), to Seville, and Hitler added to them a professional squadron from the Luftwaffe (2JG/88) with about 24 planes. All these planes had the Nationalist

Spanish insignia painted on them, but were flown by Italian and German nationals. The backbone of Franco's air force in those days was the Italian SM.79 and SM.81 bombers, the biplane Fiat CR.32 fighter and the German Junkers Ju 52 cargo- bomber and the Heinkel He 51 biplane fighter.

On the 21st of September, with the head of the column at the town of Maqueda (some 80 km away from Madrid), Franco ordered a detour to free the besieged garrison at the Alcázar of Toledo, which was achieved on the 27th of September. This controversial decision gave the Popular Front time to strengthen its defences in Madrid and hold the city that year, but with Soviet support. Kennan alleges that once Stalin had decided to assist the Spanish Republicans, the operation was put in place with remarkable speed and energy. The first load of arms and tanks arrived as early as the 26th of September and was secretly unloaded at night. Advisers accompanied the armaments. Soviet officers were in effective charge of military operations on the Madrid front. Kennan believes that this operation was originally conducted in good faith with no other purpose than saving the Republic.

Hitler's policy for Spain was shrewd and pragmatic. The minutes of a conference with his foreign minister and army chiefs at the Reich Chancellery in Berlin on the 10th of November 1937 summarised his views on foreign policy regarding the Spanish Civil War: "On the other hand, a 100 percent victory for Franco was not desirable either, from the German point of view; rather were we interested in a continuance of the war and in the keeping up of the tension in the Mediterranean." Hitler distrusted Franco; according to the comments he made at the conference he wanted the war to continue, but he did not want Franco to achieve total victory. He felt that with Franco in undisputed control of Spain, the possibility of Italy intervening further or of its continuing to occupy the Balearic Islands would be prevented.

By February 1937 the Soviet Union's military help started to taper off, to be replaced by limited economic aid. The designated leader of the uprising, General José Sanjurjo, died on 20 July 1936 in a plane crash. In the nationalist zone, "political life ceased". Initially, only military command mattered: this was divided into regional commands (Emilio Mola in the North, Gonzalo Queipo de Llano in Seville commanding Andalucia, Franco with an independent command, and Miguel Cabanellas in Zaragoza commanding Aragon). The Spanish Army of Morocco was itself split into two columns, one commanded by General Juan Yagüe and the other commanded by Colonel José Varela.

From the 24th of July a coordinating junta, the National Defence Junta, was established, based at Burgos. Nominally led by Cabanellas, as the most senior general, it initially included Mola, three other generals, and two colonels; Franco was later added in early August. On the 21ST of September it was decided that Franco was to be commander-in-chief (this unified command was opposed only by Cabanellas), and, after some discussion, with no more than a lukewarm agreement from Queipo de Llano and from Mola, also head of government. He was, doubtlessly, helped to this primacy by the fact that, in late July, Hitler had decided that all of Germany's aid to the Nationalists would go to Franco.

Mola had been somewhat discredited as the main planner of the attempted coup that had now degenerated into a civil war, and was strongly identified with the Carlist monarchists and not at all with the Falange, a party with Fascist leanings and connections ("phalanx", a far-right

Spanish political party founded by José Antonio Primo de Rivera), nor did he have good relations with Germany. Queipo de Llano and Cabanellas had both previously rebelled against the dictatorship of General Miguel Primo de Rivera and were therefore discredited in some nationalist circles, and Falangist leader José Antonio Primo de Rivera was in prison in Alicante (he would be executed a few months later). The desire to keep a place open for him prevented any other Falangist leader from emerging as a possible head of state. Franco's previous aloofness from politics meant that he had few active enemies in any of the factions that needed to be placated, and he had also cooperated in recent months with both Germany and Italy.

On the 1st of October 1936, in Burgos, Franco was publicly proclaimed as Generalísimo of the National army and Jefe del Estado (Head of State). When Mola was killed in another air accident a year later on the 2nd of June 1937 which some believe was an assassination, no military leader was left from those who had organised the conspiracy against the Republic between 1933 and 1935.

Franco personally guided military operations from this time until the end of the war. Franco himself was not a strategic genius, but he was very effective at organisation, administration, logistics and diplomacy. After the failed assault on Madrid in November 1936, Franco settled on a piecemeal approach to winning the war, rather than bold manoeuvring. As with his decision to relieve the garrison at Toledo, this approach has been subject of some debate: some of his decisions, such as in June 1938 when he preferred to advance towards Valencia instead of Catalonia, remain particularly controversial from a military strategic viewpoint. Valencia, Castellon and Alicante saw the last Republican troops defeated by Franco.

Although both Germany and Italy provided military

support to Franco, the degree of influence of both powers on his direction of the war seems to have been very limited. Nevertheless, the Italian troops, despite not always being effective, were present in most of the large operations in large numbers. Germany sent insignificant numbers of combat personnel to Spain, but aided the Nationalists with technical instructors and modern matériel; including some 200 tanks and 600 aircraft which helped the Nationalist air force dominate the skies for most of the war.

Franco's direction of the German and Italian forces was limited, particularly in the direction of the Condor Legion, but he was by default their supreme commander, and they declined to interfere in the politics of the Nationalist zone. For reasons of prestige it was decided to continue assisting Franco until the end of the war, and Italian and German troops paraded on the day of the final victory in Madrid.

The Nationalist victory could be accounted for by various factors: the Popular Front government had reckless policies in the weeks prior to the war, where it ignored potential dangers and alienated the opposition, encouraging more people to join the rebellion, while the rebels had superior military cohesion, with Franco providing the necessary leadership to consolidate power and unify the various rightist factions. His foreign diplomacy secured military aid from Italy and Germany and, by some accounts, helped keep Britain and France out of the war.

The rebels made effective use of a smaller navy, acquiring the most powerful ships in the Spanish fleet and maintaining a functional officer corp, while Republican sailors had assassinated a large number of their naval officers who sided with the rebels in 1936, as at Cartagena, and El Ferrol. The Nationalists used their ships aggressively to pursue the opposition, in contrast to the largely passive naval strategy of the Republicans.

Not only did the Nationalists receive more foreign aid to sustain their war effort, but there is evidence that they made more efficient use of such aid. They augmented their forces with arms captured from the Republicans, and successfully integrated over half of Republican prisoners of war into the Nationalist army. The rebels were able to build a larger air force and make more effective use of their air force, particularly in supporting ground operations and bombing; and generally enjoyed air superiority from mid-1937 onwards; this air power contributed greatly to the Nationalist victory.

The Republicans were subject to disunity and infighting, and were hampered by the destructive consequences of the revolution in the Republican zone: mobilisation was impeded, the Republican image was harmed abroad in democracies, and the campaign against religion aroused overwhelming and unwavering Catholic support for the Nationalists.

On the 19th of April 1937, Franco and Serrano Súñer, with the acquiescence of Generals Mola and Quiepo de Llano, forcibly merged the ideologically distinct national-syndicalist Falange and the Carlist monarchist parties into one party under his rule, dubbed Falange Española Tradicionalista y de las Juntas de Ofensiva Nacional-Sindicalista which became the only legal party in 1939.

Unlike some other fascist movements, the Falangists had developed an official program in 1934, the "Twenty-Seven Points". In 1937, Franco assumed as the tentative doctrine of his regime 26 out of the original 27 points. Franco made himself jefe nacional (National Chief) of the new FET (Falange Española Tradicionalista; Traditionalist Spanish Phalanx) with a secretary, Political Junta and

National Council to be named subsequently by himself. Five days later on the 24th of April the raised-arm salute of the Falange was made the official salute of the Nationalist regime. Also in 1937 the Marcha Real ("Royal March") was restored by decree as the national anthem in the Nationalist zone. It was opposed by the Falangists, who associated it with the monarchy and boycotted it when it was played, often singing their own anthem, Cara al Sol (Facing the Sun) instead. By 1939 the fascist style prevailed, with ritual rallying calls of "Franco, Franco, Franco."

Franco's advisor on Falangist party matters, Ramón Serrano Súñer, who was the brother-in-law of his wife Carmen Polo, and a group of Serrano Súñer's followers dominated the FET JONS, and strove to increase the party's power. Serrano Súñer tried to move the party in a more fascist direction by appointing his acolytes to important positions, and the party became the leading political organization in Francoist Spain. The FET JONS failed to establish a fascist party regime, however, and was relegated to subordinate status. Franco placed the Carlist Manuel Fal Condé under house arrest and imprisoned hundreds of old Falangists, the so-called "old shirts" (camisas viejas), including the party leader Manuel Hedilla, to help secure his political future. Franco also appeased the Carlists by exploiting the Republicans' anti-clericalism in his propaganda, in particular concerning the "Martyrs of the war". While the Republican forces presented the war as a struggle to defend the Republic against fascism, Franco depicted himself as the defender of "Catholic Spain" against "Atheist Communism".

By early 1939 only Madrid and a few other areas remained under control of the government forces. On the 27th of February Chamberlain's Britain and Daladier's

France officially recognised the Franco regime. On the 28th of March 1939, with the help of pro-Franco forces inside the city (the "fifth column" General Mola had mentioned in propaganda broadcasts in 1936), Madrid fell to the Nationalists. The next day, Valencia, which had held out under the guns of the Nationalists for close to two years, also surrendered. Victory was proclaimed on the 1st of April 1939, when the last of the Republican forces surrendered. On the same day, Franco placed his sword upon the altar of a church and vowed to never take it up again unless Spain itself was threatened with invasion.

Although Germany had recognised the Franco Government, Franco's policy towards Germany was extremely cautious until spectacular German victories at the beginning of the Second World War. An early indication that Franco was going to keep his distance from Germany soon proved true. A rumoured state visit by Franco to Germany did not take place and a further rumour of a visit by Goering to Spain, after he had enjoyed a cruise in the Western Mediterranean, again did not materialise. Instead Goering had to return to Berlin.

During the Civil War and in the aftermath, a period known as the White Terror took place. This saw mass executions of Republican and other Nationalist enemies, standing in contrast to the war-time Red Terror. Historical analysis and investigations estimate the number of executions by the Franco regime during this time to be between 100,000 and 200,000 killed. Recent searches conducted with parallel excavations of mass graves in Spain by the Association for the Recovery of Historical Memory (Asociación para la Recuperación de la Memoria Histórica), ARMH) estimate that more than 35,000 people killed by the nationalist side are still missing in mass graves.

Despite the end of the war, Spanish guerrillas exiled in

France, and known as the Maquis", continued to resist Franco in the Pyrenees, carrying out sabotage and robberies against the Francoist regime. Several exiled Republicans also fought in the French resistance against the German occupation in Vichy France during World War II. In 1944, a group of republican veterans from the French resistance invaded the Val d'Aran in northwest Catalonia, but were quickly defeated. The activities of the Maquis continued well into the 1950s.

The end of the war led to hundreds of thousands of exiles, mostly to France, but also to Mexico, Chile, Cuba, and the United States. On the other side of the Pyrenees, refugees were confined in internment camps in France, such as Camp Gurs or Camp Vernet, where 12,000 Republicans were housed in squalid conditions (mostly soldiers from the Durruti Division. The 17,000 refugees housed in Gurs were divided into four categories: Brigadists, pilots, Gudaris and ordinary "Spaniards". The Gudaris (Basques) and the pilots easily found local backers and jobs, and were allowed to quit the camp, but the farmers and ordinary people, who could not find relations in France, were encouraged by the French government, in agreement with the Francoist government, to return to Spain. The great majority did so and were turned over to the Francoist authorities in Irún. From there they were transferred to the Miranda de Ebro camp for "purification" according to the Law of Political Responsibilities. After the proclamation by Marshal Philippe Pétain of the Vichy France regime, the refugees became political prisoners, and the French police attempted to round up those who had been liberated from the camp. Along with other "undesirables", they were sent to the Drancy internment camp before being deported to Nazi Germany. 5,000 Spaniards thus died in Mauthausen concentration camp. The

Chilean poet Pablo Neruda, who had been named by the Chilean President Pedro Aguirre Cerda special consul for immigration in Paris, was given responsibility for what he called "the noblest mission I have ever undertaken": shipping more than 2,000 Spanish refugees, who had been housed by the French in squalid camps, to Chile on an old cargo ship, the Winnipeg.

In September 1939, World War II began. Franco had received important support from Adolf Hitler and Benito Mussolini during the Spanish Civil War, and he had signed the Anti-Comintern Pact. He made pro-Axis speeches, while offering various kinds of support to Italy and Germany. His spokesman Antonio Tovar commented at a Paris conference entitled 'Bolshevism versus Europe' that "Spain aligned itself definitively on the side of...National Socialist Germany and Fascist Italy." However, Franco was reluctant to enter the war due to Spain recovering from its recent civil war and instead pursued a policy of "non- belligerence".

On the 23rd of October 1940, Hitler and Franco met in Hendaye, France to discuss the possibility of Spain's entry on the side of the Axis. Franco's demands, including large supplies of food and fuel, as well as Spanish control of Gibraltar and French North Africa, proved too much for Hitler. At the time Hitler did not want to risk damaging his relations with the new Vichy French government. An oft-cited remark attributed to Hitler is that the German leader said that he would rather have some of his own teeth pulled out than to have to personally deal further with Franco.

Some historians argue that Franco made demands he knew Hitler would not accede to, in order to stay out of the war. Other historians argue that Franco, as the leader of a destroyed and bankrupt country in chaos following a brutal three-year civil war, simply had little to offer the Axis and that the Spanish armed forces were not ready for a major war. It has also been suggested that Franco decided not to join the war after the resources he requested from Hitler in October 1940 were not forthcoming.

Franco allowed Spanish soldiers to volunteer to fight in the German Army against the Soviet Union (the Blue Division), but forbade Spaniards to fight in the West against the democracies. Franco's common ground with Hitler was particularly weakened by Hitler's attempts to manipulate Christianity, which went against Franco's fervent commitment to defending Catholicism. Contributing to the disagreement was an ongoing dispute over German mining rights in Spain.

In the winter of 1940 and 1941, Franco toyed with the idea of a "Latin Bloc" formed by Spain, Portugal, Vichy France, the Vatican, and Italy, without much consequence. Franco had cautiously decided to enter the war on the Axis side in June 1940, and to prepare his people for war, an anti-British and anti-French campaign was launched in the Spanish media that demanded French Morocco, Cameroon and Gibraltar. On the 19th of June 1940, Franco pressed along a message to Hitler saying he wanted to enter the war, but Hitler was annoyed at Franco's demand for the French colony of Cameroon, which had been German before World War I, and which Hitler was planning on taking back for Plan Z. Franco seriously considered blocking allied access to the Mediterranean Sea by invading British-held Gibraltar, but he abandoned the idea after learning that the plan would have likely failed due to Gibraltar being too heavily defended. In addition, declaring war on the UK and its allies would no doubt give them an opportunity to capture both the Canary Islands and Spanish Morocco, as well as possibly launch an invasion of mainland Spain itself. Franco was aware that his air force would be quickly defeated if going into action against the Royal Air Force, and the Royal Navy would easily be able to destroy Spain's small navy and blockade the entire Spanish coast to prevent imports of crucial materials such as oil. Spain depended on oil imports from the United States, which were almost certain to be cut off if Spain formally joined the Axis. Franco and Serrano Suñer held a meeting with Mussolini and Ciano in Bordighera, Italy on the 12th of February 1941. However, an affected Mussolini did not appear to be interested in Franco's help due to the defeats his forces had suffered in North Africa and the Balkans, and he even told Franco that he wished he could find any way to leave the war. When the invasion of the Soviet Union began on the 22nd of June 1941, Franco's foreign minister Ramón Serrano Suñer immediately suggested the formation of a unit of military volunteers to join the invasion. Volunteer Spanish troops fought on the Eastern Front under German command from 1941 to 1944. Some historians have argued that not all of the Blue Division were true volunteers and that Franco expended relatively small but significant resources to aid the Axis powers' battle against the Soviet Union.

After the war, the Spanish government tried to destroy all evidence of its cooperation with the Axis. In 2010, documents were discovered showing that on the 13th of May 1941, Franco ordered his provincial governors to compile a list of Jews while he negotiated an alliance with the Axis powers. Franco supplied Reichsführer-SS Heinrich Himmler, architect of the Nazis' Final Solution, with a list of 6,000 Jews in Spain. On the 14th of June 1940, Spanish forces in Morocco occupied Tangier, a city under international control, and did not leave until the war's end in 1945.

Franco personally and many in the government openly

stated that they believed there was an international conspiracy of Freemasons and Communists against Spain,
sometimes including Jews or "Judeo-Masonry" as part of
this. While under the leadership of Francisco Franco, the
Spanish government explicitly endorsed the Catholic
Church as the religion of the nation state and did not
endorse liberal ideas such as religious pluralism or separation of Church and State found in the Republican Constitution of 1931. Following the Second World War, the
government enacted the "Spanish Bill of Rights" (Fuero de
los Españoles), which extended the right to private worship
of non-Catholic religions, including Judaism, though it
did not permit the erection of religious buildings for this
practice and did not allow non-Catholic public ceremonies.

With the pivot of Spain's foreign policy towards the
United States during the Cold War, the situation changed
with the 1967 Law on Religious Freedom, which granted
full public religious rights to non-Catholics. The overthrow of Catholicism as the explicit state religion of Spain
and the establishment of state- sponsored religious pluralism would be realized in Spain in 1978, with the new Constitution of Spain, three years after Franco's death.

On the 26th of July 1947, Franco proclaimed Spain a
monarchy, but did not designate a monarch. This gesture
was largely done to appease the monarchists in the
Movimiento Nacional (Carlists and Alfonsists). Franco left
the throne vacant, proclaiming himself as a de facto regent
for life. At the same time, Franco appropriated many of
the privileges of a king. He wore the uniform of a Captain
General (a rank traditionally reserved for the King) and
resided in El Pardo Palace. In addition he began walking
under a canopy, and his portrait appeared on most Spanish coins and postage stamps. He also added "by the grace

of God", a phrase usually part of the styles of monarchs, to his style.

Franco initially sought support from various groups. His administration marginalised fascist ideologues in favour of technocrats, many of whom were linked with Opus Dei, who promoted economic modernisation.

According to some estimates, Franco's forces killed about 420,000 Spaniards in the theatre of war, through extrajudicial killings during the Civil War, and in state executions immediately following its end in 1939. The first decade of Franco's rule following its end saw continued repression and the killing of an undetermined number of political opponents. In 1941 the prison population of Spain was 233,000, mostly political prisoners. According to recent research, at least 35,000 official executions in the country after the war. Accounting for unofficial and random killings, and those who died during the war from execution, suicide, starvation and disease in prison, the total number is probably closer to 200,000.

By the start of the 1950s Franco's state had become less violent, but during his entire rule, non-government trade unions and all political opponents across the political spectrum, from communist and anarchist organisations to liberal democrats and Catalan or Basque separatists, were either suppressed or tightly controlled with all means, up to and including violent police repression. The Confederación Nacional del Trabajo (CNT) and the Unión General de Trabajadores (UGT) trade unions were outlawed, and replaced in 1940 by the corporatist Sindicato Vertical. The Spanish Socialist Workers' Party and the Esquerra Republicana de Catalunya (ERC) were banned in 1939, while the Communist Party of Spain (PCE) went underground. The Basque Nationalist Party (PNV) went into exile, and in 1959 the ETA armed group was created to wage a low-intensity war against Franco.

Franco's Spanish nationalism promoted a unitary national identity by repressing Spain's cultural diversity. Bullfighting and flamenco were promoted as national traditions while those traditions not considered "Spanish" were suppressed. Franco's view of Spanish tradition was somewhat artificial and arbitrary: while some regional traditions were suppressed, flamenco, an Andalucian tradition, was considered part of a larger, national identity. All cultural activities were subject to censorship, and many, such as the Sardana, the national dance of Catalonia, were plainly forbidden (often in an erratic manner). This cultural policy was relaxed over time, most notably during the late 1960s and early 1970s.

Franco also used language politics in an attempt to establish national homogeneity. He promoted the use of Castilian Spanish and suppressed other languages such as Catalan, Galician, and Basque. The legal usage of languages other than Castilian was forbidden. All government, notarial, legal and commercial documents were to be drawn up exclusively in Castilian and any documents written in other languages were deemed null and void. The usage of any other language was forbidden in schools, in advertising, and on road and shop signs. For unofficial use, citizens continued to speak these languages. This was the situation throughout the 1940s and to a lesser extent during the 1950s, but after 1960 the non-Castilian Spanish languages were freely spoken and written, and they reached bookshops and stages, although they never received official status.

The Catholic Church was upheld as the established church of the Spanish State, and it regained many of the traditional privileges which it had lost under the Republic.

Civil servants had to be Catholic, and some official jobs even required a "good behavior" statement by a priest. Civil marriages which had taken place in Republican Spain were declared null and void unless they had been confirmed by the Catholic Church.

Spain attempted to retain control of its colonies throughout Franco's rule. During the Algerian War (1954–62), Madrid became the base of the Organisation armée secrète (OAS), a right-wing French Army group which sought to preserve French Algeria. Despite this, Franco was forced to make some concessions. When French Morocco became independent in 1956, he surrendered Spanish Morocco to Morocco, retaining only a few cities (the Plazas de soberanía). The year after, Mohammed V invaded Spanish Sahara during the Ifni War (known as the "Forgotten War" in Spain). Only in 1975, with the Green March, did Morocco take control of all of the former Spanish territories in the Sahara.

In 1968, under pressure from the United Nations, Spain granted Equatorial Guinea its independence, and the following year it ceded Ifni to Morocco. Under Franco, Spain also pursued a campaign to force a negotiation on the British overseas territory of Gibraltar, and closed its border with that territory in 1969. The border would not be fully reopened until 1985.

The Civil War ravaged the Spanish economy. Infrastructure had been damaged, workers killed, and daily business severely hampered. For more than a decade after Franco's victory, the devastated economy recovered very slowly. Franco initially pursued a policy of autarky, cutting off almost all international trade. The policy had devastating effects, and the economy stagnated. Only black marketeers could enjoy an evident affluence.

When Franco replaced his ideological ministers with

the apolitical technocrats, the regime implemented several development policies that included deep economic reforms. After a recession, growth took off from 1959, creating an economic boom that lasted until 1974, and became known as the "Spanish miracle"

During the 1960s, the wealthy classes of Francoist Spain experienced further increases in wealth, particularly those who remained politically faithful, while a burgeoning middle class became visible as the "economic miracle" progressed. International firms established factories in Spain where salaries were low, company taxes very low, strikes forbidden and workers' health or state protections almost unheard of. State- owned firms like the car manufacturer SEAT, truck builder Pegaso, and oil refiner INH, massively expanded production. Furthermore, Spain was virtually a new mass market. Spain became the second-fastest growing economy in the world between 1959 and 1973, just behind Japan. By the time of Franco's death in 1975, Spain still lagged behind most of Western Europe but the gap between its per capita GDP and that of the leading Western European countries had narrowed greatly, and the country had developed a large industrialised economy.

In the late 1960s, the aging Franco decided to name a monarch to succeed his regency, but the simmering tensions between the Carlists and the Alfonsoists continued. In 1969, Franco formally nominated as his heir-apparent Prince Juan Carlos de Borbón, who had been educated by him in Spain, with the new title of Prince of Spain. This designation came as a surprise to the Carlist pretender to the throne, Prince Xavier of Bourbon-Parma, as well as to Juan Carlos's father, Juan de Borbón, the Count of Barcelona, who had a better claim to the throne, but whom Franco feared to be too liberal. However, when Juan Carlos asked Franco if he could sit in on cabinet meetings, Franco would not permit him saying that "you would do things differently." Due to the spread of democracy, excluding the Eastern Bloc, in Europe since World War II, Juan Carlos could or would not have been a dictator in the way Franco had been.

By 1973, Franco had surrendered the function of prime minister (Presidente del Gobierno), remaining only as head of state and commander in chief of the military.

As his final years progressed, tensions within the various factions of the Movimiento would consume Spanish political life, as varying groups jockeyed for position in an effort to win control of the country's future. The assassination of prime minister Luis Carrero Blanco in the 20th of December 1973 bombing by ETA eventually gave an edge to the liberalizing faction.

On the 19th of July 1974, the ageing Franco fell ill from various health problems, and Juan Carlos took over as acting head of state. Franco recovered and on the 2nd of September he resumed his duties as head of state. A year later he fell ill again, afflicted with further health problems, including a long battle with Parkinson's disease. Franco's last public appearance was on the 1st of October 1975 when, despite his gaunt and frail appearance, he gave a speech to crowds from the balcony at the Royal Palace of El Pardo in Madrid. On the 30th of October 1975 he fell into a coma and was put on life support and died a few minutes after midnight on the 20th of November 1975 from heart failure, at the age of eighty-two.

As soon as news of Franco's death was made public, the government declared thirty days of official national mourning. On the 22nd of November, Juan Carlos was proclaimed King of Spain. There was a public viewing of Franco's body at the funeral chapel opened in the Royal

Palace; a mass and a military parade were held on the day of his burial.

A mass and a military parade took place on the day of his burial, the 23rd of November 1975. As the cortège with Franco's body arrived at the Valley of the Fallen, some seventy-five thousand rightists wearing the blue shirts of the Falangists greeted it with rebel songs from the civil war and fascist salutes.. Following Franco's funeral, his widow Carmen Polo supervised the moving of crates of jewellery, antiques, artworks, and Franco's papers to the family's various estates in Spain or to safe havens in foreign countries. The family remained extremely wealthy after his death.

Idi Amin

Idi Amin was a Ugandan military officer and politician who served as the third president of Uganda from 1971 to 1979. He ruled as a military dictator and is considered one of the most brutal despots in modern world history.

Idi Amin was born in Koboko in what is now northwest Uganda to a Kakwa father and Lugbara mother. In 1946, he joined the King's African Rifles of the British Colonial Army as a cook. He rose to the rank of lieutenant, taking part in British actions against Somali rebels and then the Mau Mau Uprising in Kenya. Uganda gained independence from the United Kingdom in 1962, and Idi Amin remained in the army, rising to the position of major and being appointed commander of the Uganda Army in 1965. He became aware that Ugandan President Milton Obote was planning to arrest him for misappropriating army funds, so he launched the 1971 Ugandan coup d'état and declared himself president.

During his years in power, Idi Amin shifted from being

a pro-Western ruler enjoying considerable support from Israel to being backed by Libya's Muammar Gaddafi, Zaire's Mobutu Sese Seko, the Soviet Union, and East Germany. In 1972, Idi Amin expelled Asians, a majority of whom were Indian-Ugandans, leading India to sever diplomatic relations with his regime. In 1975, Idi Amin became the chairman of the Organisation of African Unity (OAU), a Pan-Africanist group designed to promote solidarity among African states. Uganda was a member of the United Nations Commission on Human Rights from 1977 to 1979. The United Kingdom broke diplomatic relations with Uganda in 1977, and Idi Amin declared that he had defeated the British and added "CBE" to his title for "Conqueror of the British Empire".

As Idi Amin's rule progressed into the late 1970s, there was increased unrest against his persecution of certain ethnic groups and political dissidents, along with Uganda's very poor international standing due to Idi Amin's support for the terrorist hijackers in Operation Entebbe. He then attempted to annex Tanzania's Kagera Region in 1978. The Tanzanian president Julius Nyerere ordered his troops to invade Uganda in response. Tanzanian Army and rebel forces successfully captured Kampala in 1979 and ousted Idi Amin from power. Idi Amin went into exile, first in Libya, then Iraq, and finally in Saudi Arabia, where he lived until his death in 2003.

Idi Amin's rule was characterised by rampant human rights abuses, including political repression, ethnic persecution and extrajudicial killings, as well as nepotism, corruption, and gross economic mismanagement. International observers and human rights groups estimate that between 100,000 and 500,000 people were killed under his regime.

Idi Amin joined the British King's African Rifles in 1946 as an assistant cook, while at the same time receiving military training until 1947. He was transferred to Kenya for infantry service as a private in 1947, and served in the 21st KAR infantry battalion in Gilgil, Kenya Colony until 1949. That year, his unit was deployed to northern Kenya to fight against Somali rebels. In 1952, his brigade was deployed against the Mau Mau rebels in Kenya. He was promoted to corporal the same year, then to sergeant in 1953.

In 1959, Idi Amin was made Effendi class 2 (Warrant Officer), the highest rank possible for a black African in the colonial British military of that time. Idi Amin returned to Uganda the same year and received a short-service commission as a lieutenant on the 15th of July 1961, becoming one of the first two Ugandans to become commissioned officers. He was assigned to quell the cattle rustling between Uganda's Karamojong and Kenya's Turkana nomads. According to one researcher, Idi Amin's outlook, behaviour and strategies of communication were strongly influenced by his experiences in the colonial military. This included his direct and hands-on leadership style which would eventually contribute to his popularity among certain parts of Ugandan society.

In 1962, following Uganda's independence from the United Kingdom, Idi Amin was promoted to captain and then, in 1963, to major. He was appointed Deputy Commander of the Army in 1964 and, the following year, to Commander of the Army. In 1970, he was promoted to commander of all the armed forces.

Idi Amin was an athlete during his time in both the British and Uganda Army. At 1.93 metres tall and powerfully built, he was the Ugandan light heavyweight boxing champion from 1951 to 1960, as well as a swimmer. Idi Amin was also a formidable rugby forward, although one officer said of him: "Idi Amin is a splendid type and a good rugby player, but virtually bone from the neck up, and needs things explained in words of one letter". In the 1950s, he played for Nile RFC.

In 1965, Prime Minister Milton Obote and Idi Amin were implicated in a deal to smuggle ivory and gold into Uganda from the Democratic Republic of the Congo. The deal, as later alleged by General Nicholas Olenga, an associate of the former Congolese leader Patrice Lumumba, was part of an arrangement to help troops opposed to the Congolese government trade ivory and gold for arms supplies secretly smuggled to them by Idi Amin. In 1966, the Ugandan Parliament demanded an investigation. Obote imposed a new constitution abolishing the ceremonial presidency held by Kabaka (King) Mutesa II of Buganda, and declared himself executive president. He promoted Idi Amin to colonel and army commander. Idi Amin led an attack on the Kabaka's palace and forced Mutesa into exile to the United Kingdom.

Idi Amin began recruiting members of Kakwa, Lugbara, South Sudanese, and other ethnic groups from the West Nile area bordering South Sudan. The South Sudanese had been residents in Uganda since the early 20th century, having come from South Sudan to serve the colonial army. Many African ethnic groups in northern Uganda inhabit both Uganda and South Sudan; allegations persist that Idi Amin's army consisted mainly of South Sudanese.

Eventually a rift developed between Idi Amin and Obote, exacerbated by the support Idi Amin had built within the Uganda Army by recruiting from the West Nile region, his involvement in operations to support the rebellion in southern Sudan and an attempt on Obote's life in 1969. In October 1970, Obote took control of the armed forces, reducing Idi Amin from his months- old post of commander of all the armed forces to that of the commander of the Uganda Army.

Having learned that Obote was planning to arrest him for misappropriating army funds, Idi Amin seized power in a military coup on the 25th of January 1971, while Obote was attending a Commonwealth summit meeting in Singapore. Troops loyal to Idi Amin sealed off Entebbe International Airport and took Kampala. Soldiers surrounded Obote's residence and blocked major roads. A broadcast on Radio Uganda accused Obote's government of corruption and preferential treatment of the Lango region. Cheering crowds were reported in the streets of Kampala after the radio broadcast. Idi Amin, who presented himself a soldier, not a politician, declared that the military government would remain only as a caretaker regime until new elections, which would be held when the situation was normalised. He promised to release all political prisoners.

Idi Amin held a state funeral in April 1971 for Edward Mutesa, former king (kabaka) of Buganda and president who had died in exile; freed many political prisoners; and reiterated his promise to hold free and fair elections to return the country to democratic rule in the shortest period possible.

On the 2nd of February 1971, one week after the coup, Idi Amin declared himself President of Uganda, Commander-in-Chief of the Armed Forces, Uganda Army Chief of Staff, and Chief of Air Staff. He suspended certain provisions of the Ugandan constitution, and soon instituted an Advisory Defence Council composed of military officers with himself as the chairman. Idi Amin placed military tribunals above the system of civil law, appointed soldiers to top government posts and government- owned corporations, and informed the newly inducted civilian cabinet ministers that they would be subject to military courtesy.

Idi Amin ruled by decree; over the course of his rule he issued approximately thirty decrees.   .

Idi Amin renamed the presidential lodge in Kampala from Government House to "The Command Post". He disbanded the General Service Unit, an intelligence agency created by the previous government, and replaced it with the State Research Bureau. SRB headquarters at the Kampala suburb of Nakasero became the scene of torture and capital punishment over the next few years. Other agencies used to persecute dissenters included the military police and the Public Safety Unit. Obote took refuge in Tanzania, having been offered sanctuary there by the Tanzanian President Julius Nyerere. Obote was soon joined by 20,000 Ugandan refugees fleeing Idi Amin. The exiles attempted but failed to regain Uganda in 1972, through a poorly organised coup attempt.

Idi Amin retaliated against the attempted invasion by Ugandan exiles in 1972, by purging the Uganda Army of Obote supporters, predominantly those from the Acholi and Lango ethnic groups. In July 1971, Lango and Acholi soldiers had been massacred in the Jinja and Mbarara barracks. By early 1972, some 5,000 Acholi and Lango soldiers, and at least twice as many civilians, had disappeared. The victims soon came to include members of other ethnic groups, religious leaders, journalists, artists, senior bureaucrats, judges, lawyers, students and intellectuals, criminal suspects, and foreign nationals. In this atmosphere of violence, many other people were killed for criminal motives or simply at will. Bodies were often dumped into the River Nile.

The killings, motivated by ethnic, political, and financial factors, continued throughout Idi Amin's eight years in control. The exact number of people killed is unknown. The International Commission of Jurists estimated the death toll at no fewer than 80,000 and more likely around 300,000. An estimate compiled by exile organisations with the help of Amnesty International puts the number killed at half a million.

Among the most prominent people killed were Benedicto Kiwanuka, a former prime minister and chief justice; Janani Luwum, the Anglican archbishop; Joseph Mubiru, the former governor of the central bank of Uganda; Frank Kalimuzo, the vice-chancellor of Makerere University; Byron Kawadwa, a prominent playwright; and two of Idi Amin's own cabinet ministers, Erinayo Wilson Oryema and Charles Oboth Ofumbi. Idi Amin recruited his followers from his own ethnic group, the Kakwas, along with South Sudanese. By 1977, these three groups formed 60 percent of the 22 top generals and 75 percent of the cabinet. Similarly, Muslims formed 80 percent and 87.5 percent of these groups even though they were only five percent of the population. This helps explain why Idi Amin survived eight attempted coups. The Uganda Army grew from 10,000 to 25,000 by 1978. Idi Amin's military was largely a mercenary force. Half the soldiers were South Sudanese and 26 percent Congolese, with only 24 percent being Ugandan, mostly Muslim and Kakwa. In August 1972, Idi Amin declared what he called an "economic war", a set of policies that included the expropriation of properties owned by Asians and Europeans. Uganda's 80,000 Asians were mostly from the Indian subcontinent and born in the country, their ancestors having come to Uganda in search of prosperity when India was still a British colony. Many owned businesses, including large-scale enterprises, which formed the backbone of the Ugandan economy.

On the 4th of August 1972, Idi Amin issued a decree ordering the expulsion of the 50,000 Asians who were

British passport holders. This was later amended to
include all 60,000 Asians who were not Ugandan citizens.
Around 30,000 Ugandan Asians emigrated to the UK.
Others went to Commonwealth countries such as Australia, South Africa, Canada, and Fiji, or to India, Kenya,
Pakistan, Sweden, Tanzania, and the United States of
America. Idi Amin expropriated businesses and properties
belonging to the Asians and the Europeans and handed
them over to his supporters. Without the experienced
owners and proprietors, businesses were mismanaged and
many industries collapsed from lack of operational expertise and maintenance. This proved disastrous for the
already declining Ugandan economy. At the time, Asians
accounted for 90% of the country's tax revenue; with their
removal, Idi Amin's administration lost a large chunk of
government revenue and the economy all but collapsed.

In 1975, Emmanuel Blayo Wakhweya, Idi Amin's
finance minister and longest-serving cabinet member at
the time, defected to London. This prominent defection
helped Henry Kyemba, Idi Amin's health minister and a
former official of the first Obote regime, to defect in 1977
and resettle in the UK. Kyemba wrote and published "A
State of Blood", the first insider exposé of Idi Amin's rule.

Initially, Idi Amin was supported by Western powers
such as Israel, West Germany, and, in particular, Great
Britain. During the late 1960s, Obote's move to the left,
which included his Common Man's Charter and the
nationalisation of 80 British companies, had made the
West worried that he would pose a threat to Western capitalist interests in Africa and make Uganda an ally of the
Soviet Union. Idi Amin, who had served with the King's
African Rifles and taken part in Britain's suppression of the
Mau Mau uprising prior to Ugandan independence, was
known by the British as being intensely loyal to Britain.

This made him an obvious choice as Obote's successor. Although some have claimed that Idi Amin was being groomed for power as early as 1966, the plotting by the British and other Western powers began in earnest in 1969, after Obote had begun his nationalisation programme.

Throughout the first year of his presidency, Idi Amin received key military and financial support from the United Kingdom and Israel. In July 1971 he visited both countries and asked for advanced military equipment, but the states refused to provide hardware unless the Ugandan government paid for it. Idi Amin decided to seek foreign support elsewhere and in February 1972 he visited Libya. Idi Amin denounced Zionism, and in return Libyan leader Muammar Gaddafi pledged Uganda an immediate twenty-five-million-dollar loan to be followed by more lending from the Libyan–Ugandan Development Bank. Over the following months Idi Amin successively removed Israeli military advisers from his government, expelled all other Israeli technicians, and finally broke diplomatic relations. Gaddafi also mediated a resolution to longstanding Ugandan–Sudanese tensions, with Idi Amin agreeing to stop backing Anyanya rebels in southern Sudan and instead recruit the former guerilla fighters into his army.

Following the expulsion of Ugandan Asians in 1972, most of whom were of Indian descent, India severed diplomatic relations with Uganda. The same year, as part of his "economic war", Idi Amin broke diplomatic ties with the United Kingdom and nationalised all British-owned businesses. The United Kingdom and Israel ceased all trade with Uganda, but this commercial gap was quickly filled by Libya, the United States, and the Soviet Union.

The Soviet Union grew interested in Uganda as a

strategic counterbalance to perceived Chinese influence in Tanzania and Western influence in Kenya. It dispatched a military mission to Uganda in November 1973. While it could not supply the financial level available from the Western powers, the Soviet Union opted to provide Idi Amin with military hardware in exchange for his support. The Soviet Union quickly became Idi Amin's largest arms supplier, sending Uganda tanks, jets, artillery, missiles, and small arms. By 1975, it was estimated that the Soviets had provided Idi Amin's government with twelve million dollars in economic assistance and forty-eight-million dollars in arms. Idi Amin also sent several thousand Ugandans to Eastern Bloc countries for military, intelligence, and technical training, especially Czechoslovakia. East Germany was involved in the General Service Unit and the State Research Bureau, the two agencies that were most notorious for terror.

In June 1976, Idi Amin allowed an Air France airliner from Tel Aviv to Paris hijacked by two members of the Popular Front for the Liberation of Palestine – External Operations (PFLP-EO) and two members of the German Revolutionäre Zellen to land at Entebbe Airport. The hijackers were joined there by three more. Soon after, 156 non-Jewish hostages who did not hold Israeli passports were released and flown to safety, while eighty-three Jews and Israeli citizens, as well as twenty others who refused to abandon them continued to be held hostage. In the subsequent Israeli rescue operation, codenamed Operation Thunderbolt (popularly known as Operation Entebbe), on the night of 3rd to 4th of July 1976, a group of Israeli commandos flew in from Israel and seized control of Entebbe Airport, freeing nearly all the hostages. Three hostages died during the operation and ten were wounded; seven hijackers, about forty-five Ugandan soldiers, and one Israeli soldier were killed. A fourth hostage, an elderly Jewish Englishwoman who had been taken to Mulago Hospital in Kampala before the rescue operation, was subsequently murdered in reprisal. The incident further soured Uganda's international relations, leading the United Kingdom to close its High Commission in Uganda. In retaliation for Kenya's assistance in the raid, Idi Amin also ordered the killing of hundreds of Kenyans living in Uganda.

Uganda under Idi Amin embarked on a large military build-up, which raised concerns in Kenya. Early in June 1975, Kenyan officials impounded a large convoy of Soviet-made arms en route to Uganda at the port of Mombasa. Tension between Uganda and Kenya reached its climax in February 1976, when Idi Amin announced that he would investigate the possibility that parts of southern Sudan and western and central Kenya, up to within 32 kilometres (20 mi) of Nairobi, were historically a part of colonial Uganda. The Kenyan Government responded with a stern statement that Kenya would not part with "a single inch of territory". Idi Amin backed down after the Kenyan army deployed troops and armoured personnel carriers along the Kenya–Uganda border. Idi Amin's relations with Rwanda were tense, and during his tenure he repeatedly jeopardized its economy by denying its commercial vehicles transit to Mombasa and made multiple threats to bomb Kigali.

In January 1977 Idi Amin appointed General Mustafa Adrisi Vice President of Uganda. That year, a split in the Uganda Army developed between supporters of Idi Amin and soldiers loyal to Adrisi, who held significant power in the government and wanted to purge foreigners, particularly Sudanese, from the military. The growing dissatisfaction in the Uganda Army was reflected by frequent coup attempts; Idi Amin was even wounded during one of them, namely Operation Mafuta Mingi in June 1977. By 1978, the number of Idi Amin's supporters and close associates had shrunk significantly, and he faced increasing dissent from the populace within Uganda as the economy and infrastructure collapsed as a result of the years of neglect and abuse. After the killings of Bishop Luwum and ministers Oryema and Oboth Ofumbi in 1977, several of Idi Amin's ministers defected or fled into exile. In early 1978, Adrisi was severely injured in a car accident and flown to Cairo for treatment. While he was there, Idi Amin stripped him of his positions as Minister of Defence and Minister of Home Affairs and denounced him for retiring senior prison officials without his knowledge. Idi Amin then proceeded to purge several high-ranking officials from his government and took personal control of several ministerial portfolios. The shakeup caused political unrest and especially angered Adrisi's followers, who believed that the car accident was a failed assassination attempt.

In November 1978, troops loyal to Adrisi mutinied. Idi Amin sent troops against the mutineers, some of whom had fled across the Tanzanian border. Fighting consequently broke out along the Ugandan–Tanzanian border, and the Uganda Army launched an invasion of Tanzanian territory under unclear circumstances. According to several experts and politicians, Idi Amin directly ordered the invasion in an attempt to distract the Ugandan military and public from the crisis at home. Other accounts suggest, however, that Idi Amin had lost control of parts of the Uganda Army. Accordingly, the invading troops acted without his orders, and Idi Amin sanctioned the invasion post facto to save face. In any case, Idi Amin accused Tanzanian President Julius Nyerere of initiating the war against Uganda after the hostilities had erupted, and proclaimed the annexation of a section of Kagera when the Ugandan invasion initially proved to be successful. However, as Tanzania began to prepare a counter- offensive, Idi Amin reportedly realised his precarious situation, and attempted to defuse the conflict without losing face. The Ugandan President publicly suggested that he and Nyerere participate in a boxing match which, in lieu of military action, would determine the outcome of the conflict.

In January 1979, Nyerere mobilised the Tanzania People's Defence Force and counterattacked, joined by several groups of Ugandan exiles who had united as the Uganda National Liberation Army (UNLA). Idi Amin's army retreated steadily, despite military help from Libya's Muammar Gaddafi and the Palestine Liberation Organisation (PLO). The President reportedly made several trips abroad to other countries such as Saudi Arabia and Iraq during the war, attempting to enlist more foreign support. He made few public appearances in the final months of his rule, but spoke frequently on radio and television. Following a major defeat in the Battle of Lukaya, parts of the Uganda Army command reportedly urged Idi Amin to step down. He angrily refused, and declared: "If you don't want to fight, I'll do it myself." He consequently fired chief of staff Yusuf Gowon. However, Idi Amin was forced to flee the Ugandan capital by helicopter on 11 April 1979, when Kampala was captured. After a short-lived attempt to rally some remnants of the Uganda Army in eastern Uganda which reportedly included Idi Amin proclaiming the city of Jinja his country's new capital, he fled into exile. Idi Amin first escaped to Libya, where he stayed until 1980, and ultimately settled in Saudi Arabia, where the Saudi royal family allowed him sanctuary and paid him a generous subsidy in return for staying out of politics.

Idi Amin lived for a number of years on the top two floors of the Novotel Hotel on Palestine Road in Jeddah.

Brian Barron, who covered the Uganda–Tanzania War for the BBC as chief Africa correspondent, together with cameraman Mohamed Idi Amin (no relation) of Visnews in Nairobi, located Idi Amin in 1980, and secured the first interview with him since his deposition. While in exile, Idi Amin funded remnants of his army that fought in the Ugandan Bush War. Though he continued to be a controversial figure, some of Idi Amin's former followers as well as several rebel groups continued to fight in his name for decades, and occasionally advocated for his amnesty and even his restoration to Ugandan Presidency. During interviews he gave during his exile in Saudi Arabia, Idi Amin held that Uganda needed him, and never expressed remorse for the brutal nature of his regime.

In 1989, Idi Amin left his exile without authorization by the Saudi Arabian government, and flew alongside one of his sons to Zaire. There, he intended to mobilize a rebel force to reconquer Uganda which was engulfed in another civil war at the time. The rest of his family stayed in Jeddah. Despite using a false Zairean passport, Idi Amin was easily recognized upon arriving with Air Zaïre at N'djili Airport, and promptly arrested by Zairean security forces. The Zairean government reacted unfavourably to Idi Amin's arrival, and attempted to expel him from the country. At first, Saudi Arabia refused to allow him to return, as its government was deeply offended that he had "abused their hospitality" by leaving without permission. The Zairean government wanted neither to extradite Idi Amin to Uganda where the ex-president faced murder charges nor keep him in Zaire, thereby straining international relations. As a result, Idi Amin was initially expelled to Senegal from where he was supposed to be sent to Saudi Arabia, but the Senegalese government sent him back to Zaire when Saudi Arabia continued to refuse Idi Amin a visa. Following appeals by

Moroccan King Hassan II, the Saudi Arabian leadership finally relented and allowed Idi Amin to return. In return, Idi Amin had to promise to never again participate in any political or military activities or give interviews. He consequently spent the remainder of his life in Saudi Arabia.

In the final years of his life, Idi Amin reportedly ate a fruitarian diet. His daily consumption of oranges earned him the nickname "Dr Jaffa" among Saudi Arabians.

On the 19th of July 2003, Idi Amin's fourth wife, Nalongo Madina, reported that he was in a coma and near death at the King Faisal Specialist Hospital and Research Centre in Jeddah, Saudi Arabia, from kidney failure. She pleaded with the Ugandan president, Yoweri Museveni, to allow him to return to Uganda for the remainder of his life. Museveni replied that Idi Amin would have to "answer for his sins the moment he was brought back". Idi Amin's family eventually decided to disconnect life support, and Idi Amin consequently died at the hospital in Jeddah on the 16th of August 2003. He was buried in Ruwais Cemetery in Jeddah in a simple grave, without any fanfare.

Papa Doc Duvalier

François Duvalier, also known as Papa Doc, was a Haitian politician of French Martiniquan descent who served as the President of Haiti from 1957 until his death on countryside from the Magloire regime. In 1956, the Magloire government was failing, and although still in hiding, Papa Doc announced his candidacy to replace him as president. By December 1956, an amnesty was issued and Papa Doc emerged from hiding, and on the 12TH of December 1956, Magloire conceded defeat.

The two frontrunners in the 1957 campaign for the presidency were Papa Doc and Louis Déjoie, a landowner and industrialist from the north. During their campaigning, Haiti was ruled by five temporary administrations, none lasting longer than a few months. Papa Doc promised to rebuild and renew the country and rural Haiti solidly supported him as did the military. He resorted to noiriste populism, stoking the majority Afro-Haitians' irritation at being governed by the few mulatto elite, which is how he described his opponent, Déjoie. .

François Duvalier was elected president on the 22ND of September 1957. He received 679,884 votes to Déjoie's 266,992. Even in this election, however, there are multiple first-hand accounts of voter fraud and voter intimidation. Papa Doc then exiled most of the major supporters of Déjoie and had a new constitution adopted that year.

Papa Doc promoted and installed members of the black majority in the civil service and the army. In July 1958, three exiled Haitian army officers and five American mercenaries landed in Haiti and tried to overthrow Papa Doc; all were killed. Although the army and its leaders had quashed the coup attempt, the incident deepened Papa Doc's distrust of the army, an important Haitian institution over which he did not have firm control. He replaced the chief-of-staff with a more reliable officer and then proceeded to create his own power base within the army by turning the Presidential Guard into an elite corps aimed at maintaining his power. After this, Papa Doc dismissed the entire general staff and replaced it with officers who owed their positions, and their loyalty, to him.

In 1959, Papa Doc created a rural militia, the Militia of National Security Volunteers to extend and bolster support for the regime in the countryside. This force, named the Macoute, which by 1961 was twice as big as the army, never developed into a real military force but was more than just a secret police.

In the early years of his rule, Papa Doc was able to take advantage of the strategic weaknesses of his powerful opponents, mostly from the mulatto elite. These weaknesses included their inability to coordinate their actions against the regime, whose power had grown increasingly stronger. In the name of nationalism, Papa Doc expelled almost all of Haiti's foreign-born bishops, an act that earned him excommunication from the Catholic Church. In 1966, he persuaded the Holy See to allow him permission to nominate the Catholic hierarchy for Haiti. Papa Doc now exercised more power in Haiti than ever.

On the 24th of May 1959, Papa Doc suffered a massive heart attack, possibly due to an insulin overdose; he had been a diabetic since early adulthood and also suffered from heart disease and associated circulatory problems. During the heart attack, he was comatose for nine hours.

He was elected president in the 1957 general election on a populist and black nationalist platform. After thwarting a military coup d'état in 1958, his regime rapidly became more autocratic and despotic. An undercover government death squad indiscriminately killed Papa Doc's opponents. Called the Tonton Macoute, it was thought to be so pervasive that Haitians became highly fearful of expressing any form of dissent, even in private. Papa Doc further sought to solidify his rule by incorporating elements of Haitian mythology into a personality cult.

Prior to his rule, Papa Doc was a physician by profession. He graduated from the Graduate School of Public Health at the University of Michigan on a scholarship that was meant to train Black doctors from the Caribbean to take care of African-American servicemen during World

War II. Due to his profession and expertise in the medical field, he acquired the nickname "Papa Doc". He was unanimously "re-elected" in a 1961 presidential election in which he was the only candidate. Afterwards, he consolidated his power step by step, culminating in 1964 when he declared himself President for Life after another sham election, and as a result, he remained in power until his death and was succeeded by his son, Jean-Claude, who was nicknamed "Baby Doc".

Papa Doc was born in Port-au-Prince in 1907, the son of Duval Duvalier, a justice of the peace, and baker Ulyssia Abraham. He completed a degree in medicine from the University of Haiti in 1934, and served as staff physician at several local hospitals. He spent a year at the University of Michigan studying public health.

The racism and violence that occurred during the United States occupation of Haiti, which began in 1915, inspired black nationalism among Haitians and left a powerful impression on the young Papa Doc. He was also aware of the latent political power of the poor black majority and their resentment against the small mulatto (black and white mixed-race) elite. Papa Doc supported Pan-African ideals, and became involved in the négritude movement of Haitian author Jean Price-Mars, both of which led to his advocacy of Haitian Voodoo, an ethnological study of which later paid enormous political dividends for him. In 1938, Papa Doc co-founded the journal Les Griots. On the 27th of December 1939, he married Simone Duvalier (née Ovide), with whom he had four children: Marie-Denise, Nicole, Simone, and Jean-Claude.

In 1946, Papa Doc aligned himself with President Dumarsais Estimé and was appointed Director General of the National Public Health Service. In 1949, he served as Minister of Health and Labor, but when Papa Doc opposed Paul Magloire's 1950 coup d'état, he left the government and resumed practicing medicine. His practice included taking part in campaigns to prevent yaws and other diseases. In 1954, Papa Doc abandoned medicine, hiding out in Haiti's believed that he had suffered neurological damage during these events, harming his mental health and perhaps explaining his subsequent actions.

While recovering, Papa Doc left power in the hands of Clément Barbot, leader of the Tonton Macoute. Upon his return to work, Papa Doc accused Barbot of trying to supplant him as president and had him imprisoned. In April 1963, Barbot was released and began plotting to remove Papa Doc from office by kidnapping his children. The plot failed and Papa Doc then ordered a nationwide search for Barbot and his fellow conspirators. During the search, Papa Doc was told that Barbot had transformed himself into a black dog, which prompted Papa Doc to order that all black dogs in Haiti be put to death. The Tonton Macoute captured and killed Barbot in July 1963. In other incidents, Papa Doc ordered the head of an executed rebel packed in ice and brought to him so he could commune with the dead man's spirit. Peepholes were carved into the walls of the interrogation chambers, through which Papa Doc watched Haitian detainees being tortured and submerged in baths of sulfuric acid; sometimes, he was in the room during the torture.. In 1961, Papa Doc began violating the provisions of the 1957 constitution. First, he replaced the bicameral legislature with a unicameral body. Then he called a new presidential election in which he was the sole candidate, though his term was to expire in 1963 and the constitution prohibited re-election. The election was flagrantly rigged; the official tally showed a total of 1,320,748 "yes" votes for another term for Papa Doc, with none opposed. Upon hearing the results, he proclaimed, "I accept the people's will   As a revolutionary, I have no right to disregard the will of the people". The New York Times commented, "Latin America has witnessed many fraudulent elections throughout its history but none has been more outrageous than the one which has just taken place in Haiti". On the 14th of June 1964, a constitutional referendum made Papa Doc "President for Life", a title previously held by seven Haitian presidents. This referendum was also blatantly rigged; an implausible 99.9% voted in favor, which should have come as no surprise since all the ballots were premarked "yes". The new document granted Papa Doc absolute powers as well as the right to name his successor.

His relationship with the United States proved difficult. In his early years, Papa Doc rebuked the United States for its friendly relations with Dominican dictator Rafael Trujillo while ignoring Haiti. The Kennedy administration was particularly disturbed by Papa Doc's repressive and totalitarian rule and allegations that he misappropriated aid money, at the time a substantial part of the Haitian budget, and a U.S. Marine Corps mission to train the Tonton Macoute. The U.S. thus halted most of its economic assistance in mid-1962, pending stricter accounting procedures, with which Papa Doc refused to comply. Papa Doc publicly renounced all aid from Washington on nationalist grounds, portraying himself as a "principled and lonely opponent of domination by a great power".

After the assassination of John F. Kennedy in November 1963, which Papa Doc later claimed resulted from a curse that he had placed on Kennedy, the U.S. eased its pressure on Papa Doc, grudgingly accepting him as a bulwark against communism. Papa Doc attempted to exploit tensions between the U.S. and Cuba, emphasizing his anti-communist credentials and Haiti's strategic location as a means of winning U.S. support.

After Fulgencio Batista, a friend of Papa Doc, was over-thrown in the Cuban Revolution, Papa Doc worried that new Cuban leader Fidel Castro would provide a safe haven for Haitian dissidents. Papa Doc attempted to win Cuba over by recognizing Castro's government by sending medicine and pardoning several political prisoners, but to no avail; from the very start of his regime, Castro gave anti-Papa Doc dissidents his full support.

Papa Doc's relationship with the neighbouring Domini-can Republic was always tense. In his early years, Papa Doc emphasized the differences between the two coun-tries. In April 1963, relations were brought to the edge of war by the political enmity between Papa Doc and Domini-can president Juan Bosch. Bosch, a leftist, provided asy-lum and support to Haitian exiles who had plotted against the Papa Doc regime. Papa Doc ordered his Presidential Guard to occupy the Dominican Embassy in Pétion-Ville, with the goal of arresting a Haitian army officer believed to have been involved in Barbot's plot to kidnap Papa Doc's children. The Dominican president reacted with outrage, publicly threatened to invade Haiti, and ordered army units to the border. However, as Dominican military commanders expressed little support for an invasion of Haiti, Bosch refrained from the invasion and sought medi-ation through the OAS.

In 1966, Papa Doc hosted the emperor of Ethiopia, Haile Selassie I, in what would be the only visit of a foreign head of state to Haiti under Papa Doc. During the visit, the two discussed bilateral agreements between their two nations and the economic shortcomings brought about by international pressure. Papa Doc awarded Haile Selassie the Necklace of the Order of Jean-Jacques Dessalines the

Great, and the emperor, in turn, bestowed upon Papa Doc the Great Necklace of the Order of the Queen of Sheba.

Papa Doc's government was one of the most repressive in the Western Hemisphere. Within the country he murdered and exiled his opponents; estimates of those killed are as high as sixty thousands. Attacks on Papa Doc from within the military were treated as especially serious. When bombs were detonated near the Presidential Palace in 1967, Papa Doc had nineteen officers of the Presidential Guard executed in Fort Dimanche. A few days later Papa Doc gave a public speech during which he read the attendance sheet with names of all nineteen officers killed. After each name, he said "absent". After reading the whole list, Papa Doc remarked that "all were shot".

Haitian communists and even suspected communists bore the brunt of the government's repression. Papa Doc targeted them to reassure the U.S. he was not communist. Papa Doc was exposed to communist and leftist ideas early in his life and rejected them. On the 28th of April 1969, Papa Doc instituted a campaign to rid Haiti of all communists. A new law declared that "Communist activities, no matter what their form, are hereby declared crimes against the security of the State." Those convicted of Communist activity were subject to execution and faced having their property confiscated.

Papa Doc employed intimidation, repression, and patronage to supplant the old mulatto elites with a new elite of his own making. Corruption, in the form of government rake-offs of industries, bribery, extortion domestic businesses, and stolen government funds, enriched the dictator's closest supporters. Most of them held sufficient power to intimidate the members of the old elite, who were gradually co-opted or eliminated. Many educated professionals fled Haiti for New York City,

Miami, Montreal, Paris and several French-speaking African countries, exacerbating an already serious lack of doctors and teachers. Some of the highly skilled professionals joined the ranks of several UN agencies to work in development in newly independent nations such as Ivory Coast, and the Congo.

The government confiscated peasant landholdings and allotted them to members of the militia, who had no official salary and made their living through crime and extortion. The dispossessed fled to the slums of the capital where they would find only meager incomes to feed themselves. Malnutrition and famine became endemic.

Nonetheless, Papa Doc enjoyed significant support among Haiti's majority black rural population, who saw in him a champion of their claims against the historically dominant mulatto elite. During his 14 years in power, he created a substantial black middle class, chiefly through government patronage. Papa Doc also initiated the development of François Papa Doc Airport, now known as Toussaint Louverture International Airport.

Papa Doc fostered his cult of personality and claimed that he was the physical embodiment of the island nation. He also revived the traditions of Voodoo, later using them to consolidate his power with his claim of being a Voodoo priest himself. In an effort to make himself even more imposing, Papa Doc deliberately modeled his image on that of Baron Samedi, one of the lwa, or spirits, of Haitian Voodoo. He often donned sunglasses in order to hide his eyes and talked with the strong nasal tone associated with the lwa. The regime's propaganda stated that "Papa Doc was one with the lwa, Jesus Christ and God himself". The most celebrated image from the time shows a standing Jesus Christ with a hand on the shoulder of a seated Papa Doc, captioned, "I have chosen him". Papa Doc declared

himself an "immaterial being" as well as "the Haitian flag"
soon after his first election. In 1964, he published a cate-
chism in which the Lord's Prayer was heavily reworded to
praise Papa Doc instead of God.

François Papa Doc Duvalier died of heart disease and
diabetes on the 21st of April 1971. His 19-year-old son
Jean-Claude Duvalier, nicknamed "Baby Doc", succeeded
him as president. On February the 8th 1986, when the
Papa Doc regime fell, a crowd attacked Papa Doc's mausoleum, throwing boulders at it, chipping off pieces from
it, and breaking open the crypt. Papa Doc's coffin was not
inside, however. A prevailing rumour in the capital,
according to The New York Times, was that his son had
removed his remains upon fleeing to the United States in
an Air Force transport plane the day before.

Pol Pot

Pol Pot was a Cambodian revolutionary, dictator, and
politician who ruled Cambodia as Prime Minister of
Democratic Kampuchea between 1976 and 1979. Ideologically a Marxist– Leninist and a Khmer nationalist, he was
a leading member of Cambodia's communist movement,
the Khmer Rouge, from 1963 until 1997 and he served as
the General Secretary of the Communist Party of Kampuchea from 1963 to 1981. Under his administration,
Cambodia was converted into a one-party Communist
state.

Born as Saloth Sâr to a prosperous farmer on the 19th
of May 1925, Pol Pot was educated at some of Cambodia's
most elite schools and while in Paris during the 1940s, he
joined the French Communist Party. Returning to Cambodia in 1953, he involved himself in the Marxist–Leninist

Khmer Viet Minh organisation and its guerrilla war against King Norodom Sihanouk's newly independent government. Following the Khmer Viet Minh's 1954 retreat into Marxist–Leninist controlled North Vietnam, Pol Pot returned to Phnom Penh, working as a teacher while remaining a central member of Cambodia's Marxist–Leninist movement. In 1959, he helped formalise the movement into the Kampuchean Labour Party, which was later renamed the Communist Party of Kampuchea (CPK). To avoid state repression, in 1962 he relocated to a jungle encampment and in 1963 became the CPK's leader. In 1968, he relaunched the war against Sihanouk's government. After Lon Nol ousted Sihanouk in a 1970 coup, Pol Pot's forces sided with the deposed leader against the new government, which was bolstered by the United States military. Aided by the Viet Cong militia and North Vietnamese troops, Pol Pot's Khmer Rouge forces advanced and controlled all of Cambodia by 1975.

Pol Pot transformed Cambodia into a one-party state which he called Democratic Kampuchea. Seeking to create an agrarian socialist society that he believed would evolve into a communist society, Pol Pot's government forcibly relocated the urban population to the countryside and forced it to work on collective farms. Pursuing complete egalitarianism, money was abolished and all citizens were forced to wear the same black clothing. Mass killings of perceived government opponents, coupled with malnutrition and poor medical care, killed between one-point- five and two million people, approximately a quarter of Cambodia's population; a process which was later termed the "Cambodian Genocide". Repeated purges of the CPK generated growing discontent; by 1978 Cambodian soldiers were mounting a rebellion in the east. After several years of border clashes, the newly unified Vietnam invaded

Cambodia in December 1978, toppling Pol Pot and installing a rival Marxist–Leninist government in 1979. The Khmer Rouge retreated to the jungles near the Thai border, from where they continued to fight. In declining health, Pol Pot stepped back from many of his roles in the movement. In 1998, the Khmer Rouge commander Ta Mok placed Pol Pot under house arrest and shortly afterward, Pol Pot died.

Saddam Hussein

Saddam Hussein, born in 1937 , was an Iraqi politician who served as the fifth president of Iraq from the 16th of July 1979 until the 9th of April 2003. A leading member of the revolutionary Arab Socialist Ba'ath Party, and later, the Baghdad-based Ba'ath Party and its regional organization, the Iraqi Ba'ath Party, Saddam played a key role in the 1968 coup which brought the party to power in Iraq.

As vice president under the ailing General Ahmed Hassan al- Bakr, and at a time when many groups were considered capable of overthrowing the government, Saddam created security forces through which he tightly controlled conflicts between the government and the armed forces. In the early 1970s, Saddam nationalised the Iraq Petroleum Company and independent banks, eventually leaving the banking system insolvent due to inflation   and   bad loans. Through the 1970s, Saddam consolidated his authority over the apparatus of government as oil money helped Iraq's economy grow rapidly. Positions of power in the country were mostly filled with Sunni Arabs, a minority that made up only a fifth of the population. Saddam formally took power in 1979, although he had already been the de facto head of Iraq for several years. He suppressed several movements, particularly Shi'a and Kurdish movements which sought to overthrow the government or gain independence, respectively, and maintained power during the Iran–Iraq War and the Gulf War. He ran a repressive authoritarian govern- ment, which several analysts have described as totalitarian, although the applicability of that label has been contested. Saddam's rule was marked by numerous human rights abuses, including an estimated quarter of a million arbitrary killings, and bloody invasions of neigh- bouring Iran and Kuwait.

In 2003, a coalition led by the United States invaded Iraq to depose Saddam. US President George W. Bush and United Kingdom Prime Minister Tony Blair erro- neously accused Iraq of possessing weapons of mass destruction and having ties to al- Qaeda. Saddam's Ba'ath party was disbanded. After his capture on the 13th of December 2003, the trial of Saddam Hussein took place under the Iraqi Interim Government. On the 5th of November 2006, Saddam was convicted by an Iraqi court of crimes against humanity related to the 1982 killing of one hundred and forty-eight Iraqi Shi'a and sentenced to death by hanging. He was executed on the 30th of December 2006. Saddam was born on the 28th of April 1937 in Awja, a small village near Tikrit. Saddam's brother and father Abd al-Majid al- Tikriti both died of cancer sometime before Sassam's birth. These deaths made Saddam's mother, Subha Tulfah al-Mussallat, so depressed that she attempted to abort her pregnancy and commit suicide. Saddam eventually was taken in by an uncle. His mother remarried, and Saddam gained three half-brothers through this marriage. His stepfather, Ibrahim al-Hassan, treated Saddam harshly after his return, and beat him regularly, sometimes to wake him up. At around the age of ten, Saddam fled the family and returned to live in Baghdad with his uncle Khairallah Talfah, who became a fatherly figure to him. Talfah, the father of Saddam's future wife, was a devout Sunni Muslim and a veteran of the 1941 Anglo-Iraqi War between Iraqi nationalists and the United Kingdom, which remained a major colonial power in the region. Talfah later became the mayor of Baghdad during Saddam's time in power, until his notorious corruption compelled Saddam to force him out of office.

Later in his life, relatives from his native Tikrit became some of Saddam's closest advisors and supporters. Under the guidance of his uncle, he attended a nationalistic high school in Baghdad. After secondary school, Saddam studied at an Iraqi law school for three years, dropping out in 1957 at the age of twenty to join the revolutionary pan-Arab Ba'ath Party, of which his uncle was a supporter. During this time, Saddam apparently supported himself as a secondary school teacher. Ba'athist ideology originated in Syria and the Ba'ath Party had a large following in Syria at the time, but in 1955 there were fewer than 300 Ba'ath Party members in Iraq and it is believed that Saddam's primary reason for joining the party as opposed to the more established Iraqi nationalist parties was his familial connection to Ahmed Hassan al-Bakr and other leading Ba'athists through his uncle.

Revolutionary sentiment was characteristic of the era in Iraq and throughout the Middle East. In Iraq progressives and socialists assailed traditional political elites including colonial-era bureaucrats and landowners, wealthy merchants and tribal chiefs, and monarchists). Moreover, the pan-Arab nationalism of Gamal Abdel Nasser in Egypt profoundly influenced young Ba'athists like Saddam. The rise of Nasser foreshadowed a wave of revolutions throughout the Middle East in the 1950s and 1960s, with the collapse of the monarchies of Iraq, Egypt, and Libya. Nasser inspired nationalists throughout the Middle East by fighting the British and the French during the Suez Crisis of 1956, modernizing Egypt, and uniting the Arab world politically. His father-in-law, Khairallah Talfah, was reported to have served five years in prison for his role in fighting against Great Britain in the 1941 Iraqi coup d'état and Anglo-Iraqi War, and often mentored and told tales of his exploits to the young Saddam. In 1958, a year after Saddam had joined the Ba'ath party, army officers led by General Abd al-Karim Qasim overthrew Faisal II of Iraq in the 14th of July Revolution.

The Ba'ath Party was originally represented in Qasim's cabinet. The party turned against him for his refusal to join Gamal Abdel Nasser's United Arab Republic (UAR). To strengthen his own position within the government, Qasim created an alliance with the Iraqi Communist Party, which was opposed to any notion of pan-Arabism. Later that year, the Ba'ath Party leadership was planning to assassinate Qasim. Saddam was a leading member of the operation. At the time, the Ba'ath Party was more of an ideological experiment than a strong anti- government fighting machine. The majority of its members were either educated professionals or students, and Saddam fitted the bill. The idea of assassinating Qasim may have been Nasser's, and there is speculation that some of those who participated in the operation received training in Damascus, which was then part of the UAR. Saddam himself is not believed to have received any training outside of Iraq, as he was a late addition to the assassination team.

The assassins planned to ambush Qasim at Al-Rashid on the 7th of October 1959: one man was to kill those sitting at the back of the car, the rest killing those in front. During

the ambush it is claimed that Saddam began shooting pre-
maturely, which disorganized the whole operation.
Qasim's chauffeur was killed, and Qasim was hit in the
arm and shoulder. The assassins believed they had killed
him and quickly retreated to their headquarters, but
Qasim survived. At the time of the attack the Ba'ath Party
had fewer than one thousand members. Saddam's role in
the failed assassination became a crucial part of his public
image for decades.

Some of the plotters, including Saddam, quickly managed to leave the country for Syria, the spiritual home of
Ba'athist ideology. There Saddam was given full membership in the party. Some members of the operation were
arrested and taken into custody by the Iraqi government.
At the show trial, six of the defendants were given death
sentences; for unknown reasons the sentences were not
carried out. Aflaq, the leader of the Ba'athist movement,
organized the expulsion of leading Iraqi Ba'athist members, such as Fuad al-Rikabi, on the grounds that the party
should not have initiated the attempt on Qasim's life. At
the same time, Aflaq secured seats in the Iraqi Ba'ath leadership for his supporters, one of them being Saddam. Saddam moved from Syria to Egypt itself in February 1960,
and he continued to live there until 1963, graduating from
school in 1961 and unsuccessfully pursuing a law degree at
Cairo Law School.

Army officers with ties to the Ba'ath Party overthrew
Qasim in the Ramadan Revolution coup of February 1963.
Ba'athist leaders were appointed to the cabinet and Abdul
Salam Arif became president. Arif dismissed and arrested
the Ba'athist leaders later that year in the November 1963
Iraqi coup d'état. Being exiled in Egypt at the time, Sad-
dam played no role in the 1963 coup or the brutal anti-
communist purge that followed; although he returned to

Iraq after the coup, Saddam remained "on the fringes of the newly installed Ba'ath administration and to content himself with the minor position of a member of the Party's central bureau for peasants.

During the Qasim years, Saddam remained in Iraq following Arif's anti-Ba'athist purge in November 1963, and became involved in planning to assassinate Arif. In marked contrast to Qasim, Saddam knew that he faced no death penalty from Arif's government and knowingly accepted the risk of being arrested rather than fleeing to Syria again. Saddam was arrested in October 1964 and served approximately two years in prison before escaping in 1966. In 1966, Ahmed Hassan al-Bakr appointed him Deputy Secretary of the Regional Command. Saddam, who would prove to be a skilled organizer, revitalized the party. He was elected to the Regional Command. In September 1966, Saddam initiated an extraordinary challenge to Syrian domination of the Ba'ath Party in response to the Marxist takeover of the Syrian Ba'ath earlier that year, resulting in the Party's formalized split into two separate factions. Saddam then created a Ba'athist security service, which he alone controlled.

In July 1968, Saddam participated in a bloodless coup led by Ahmed Hassan al-Bakr that overthrew Abdul Rahman Arif, Salam Arif's brother and successor. While Saddam's role in the coup was not hugely significant Saddam planned and carried out the subsequent purge of the non-Ba'athist faction led by Prime Minister Abd ar-Razzaq an-Naif, whose support had been essential to the coup's success. According to a semi-official biography, Saddam personally led Naif at gunpoint to the plane that escorted him out of Iraq. Arif was given refuge in London and then Istanbul. Al-Bakr was named president and Saddam was named his deputy, and deputy chairman of the Ba'athist

Revolutionary Command Council. According to biographers, Saddam never forgot the tensions within the first
Ba'athist government, which formed the basis for his measures to promote Ba'ath party unity as well as his resolve
to maintain power and programs to ensure social stability.
Although Saddam was al-Bakr's deputy, he was a strong
behind-the-scenes party politician. Al-Bakr was the older
and more prestigious of the two, but by 1969 Saddam
clearly had become the moving force behind the party.

In the late 1960s and early 1970s, as vice chairman
of the Revolutionary Command Council, formally Al-
Bakr's second-in- command, Saddam built a reputation as
a progressive, effective politician. At this time, Saddam
moved up the ranks in the new government by aiding
attempts to strengthen and unify the Ba'ath party and
taking a leading role in addressing the country's major
domestic problems and expanding the party's following.
After the Ba'athists took power in 1968, Saddam focused
on attaining stability in a nation riddled with profound
tensions. Long before Saddam, Iraq had been split along
social, ethnic, religious, and economic fault lines: Sunni
versus Shi'ite, Arab versus Kurd, tribal chief versus urban
merchant, nomad versus peasant. The desire for stable
rule in a country rife with factionalism led Saddam to
pursue both massive repression and the improvement of
living standards.

Saddam actively fostered the modernization of the
Iraqi economy along with the creation of a strong security
apparatus to prevent coups within the power structure
and insurrections apart from it. Ever concerned with
broadening his base of support among the diverse elements of Iraqi society and mobilizing mass support, he
closely followed the administration of state welfare and
development programs

At the centre of this strategy was Iraq's oil. On the 1st of June 1972, Saddam oversaw the seizure of international oil interests, which, at the time, dominated the country's oil sector. A year later, world oil prices rose dramatically as a result of the 1973 energy crisis, and skyrocketing revenues enabled Saddam to expand his agenda.

Within just a few years, Iraq was providing social services that were unprecedented among Middle Eastern countries. Saddam established and controlled the "National Campaign for the Eradication of Illiteracy" and the campaign for "Compulsory Free Education in Iraq," and largely under his auspices, the government established universal free schooling up to the highest education levels; hundreds of thousands learned to read in the years following the initiation of the program. The government also supported families of soldiers, granted free hospitalization to everyone, and gave subsidies to farmers. Iraq created one of the most modernized public-health systems in the Middle East, earning Saddam an award from the United Nations Educational, Scientific and Cultural Organization (UNESCO).

With the help of increasing oil revenues, Saddam diversified the largely oil-based Iraqi economy. Saddam implemented a national infrastructure campaign that made great progress in building roads, promoting mining, and developing other industries. The campaign helped Iraq's energy industries. Electricity was brought to nearly every city in Iraq, and many outlying areas. Before the 1970s, most of Iraq's people lived in the countryside and roughly two-thirds were peasants. This number would decrease quickly during the 1970s as global oil prices helped revenues to rise from less than a half billion dollars to tens of billions of dollars and the country invested into industrial expansion.

The oil revenue benefited Saddam politically. According to The Economist, "Much as Adolf Hitler won early praise for galvanizing German industry, ending mass unemployment and building autobahns, Saddam earned admiration abroad for his deeds. He had a good instinct for what the "Arab street" demanded, following the decline in Egyptian leadership brought about by the trauma of Israel's six-day victory in the 1967 war, the death of the pan-Arabist hero, Gamal Abdul Nasser, in 1970, and the "traitorous" drive by his successor, Anwar Sadat, to sue for peace with the Jewish state.

Saddam's self-aggrandizing propaganda, with himself posing as the defender of Arabism against Jewish or Persian intruders, was heavy-handed, but consistent as a drumbeat. It helped, of course, that his mukhabarat (secret police) put dozens of Arab news editors, writers and artists on the payroll."

In 1972, Saddam signed a fifteen-year Treaty of Friendship and Cooperation with the Soviet Union. According to a known historian, the treaty upset the US-sponsored security system established as part of the Cold War in the Middle East. It appeared that any enemy of the Baghdad regime was a potential ally of the United States. In response, the US covertly financed Kurdish rebels led by Mustafa Barzani during the Second Iraqi– Kurdish War; the Kurds were defeated in 1975, leading to the forcible relocation of hundreds of thousands of Kurdish civilians.. Saddam focused on fostering loyalty to the Ba'athists in the rural areas. After nationalizing foreign oil interests, Saddam supervised the modernization of the countryside, mechanizing agriculture on a large scale, and distributing land to peasant farmers. The Ba'athists established farm cooperatives and the government also doubled expenditures for agricultural development in 1974 to 75. Saddam's welfare programs were part of a combination of "carrot and stick" tactics to enhance support for Saddam. The state-owned banks were put under his thumb. Lending was based on cronyism. Development went forward at such a fevered pitch that two million people from other Arab countries and even Yugoslavia worked in Iraq to meet the growing demand for labour.

In 1976, Saddam rose to the position of general in the Iraqi armed forces, and rapidly became the strongman of the government. As the ailing, elderly al-Bakr became unable to execute his duties, Saddam took on an increasingly prominent role as the face of the government both internally and externally. He soon became the architect of Iraq's foreign policy and represented the nation in all diplomatic situations. He was the de facto leader of Iraq some years before he formally came to power in 1979. He slowly began to consolidate his power over Iraq's government and the Ba'ath party. Relationships with fellow party members were carefully cultivated, and Saddam soon accumulated a powerful circle of support within the party.. In 1979, al-Bakr started to make treaties with Syria, also under Ba'athist leadership, that would lead to unification between the two countries. Syrian President Hafez al-Assad would become deputy leader in a union, and this would drive Saddam to obscurity. Saddam acted to secure his grip on power. He forced the ailing al-Bakr to resign on the 16th of July 1979, and formally assumed the presidency.

Saddam convened an assembly of Ba'ath party leaders on the 22nd of July 1979. During the assembly, which he ordered videotaped, Saddam claimed to have found a fifth column within the Ba'ath Party and directed Muhyi Abdel-Hussein to read out a confession and the names of sixty-eight alleged co-conspirators. These members were labelled "disloyal" and were removed from the room one by one and taken into custody. After the list was read, Saddam congratulated those still seated in the room for their past and future loyalty. The sixty-eight people arrested at the meeting were subsequently tried together and found guilty of treason; twenty-two were sentenced to execution. Other high-ranking members of the party formed the firing squad. By the 1st of August 1979, hundreds of high-ranking Ba'ath party members had been executed.

The major instruments for accomplishing this control were the paramilitary and police organizations. Beginning in 1974, Taha Yassin Ramadan, himself a Kurdish Ba'athist, a close associate of Saddam, commanded the People's Army, which had responsibility for internal security. As the Ba'ath Party's paramilitary, the People's Army acted as a counterweight against any coup attempts by the regular armed forces. In addition to the People's Army, the Department of General Intelligence was the most notorious arm of the state-security system, feared for its use of torture and assassination. Barzan Ibrahim al-Tikriti, Saddam's younger half-brother, commanded Mukhabarat. Foreign observers believed that from 1982 this department operated both at home and abroad in its mission to seek out and eliminate Saddam's perceived opponents.

Saddam was notable for using terror against his own people. The Economist described Saddam as "one of the last of the 20th century's great dictators, but not the least in terms of egotism, or cruelty, or morbid will to power." Saddam's regime brought about the deaths of at least a quarter of a million Iraqis and committed war crimes in Iran, Kuwait, and Saudi Arabia. Human Rights Watch and Amnesty International issued regular reports of widespread imprisonment and torture. Conversely, Saddam used Iraq's oil wealth to develop an extensive patronage system for the regime's supporters.

During his leadership, Saddam promoted the idea of dual nationalism which combines Iraqi nationalism and Arab nationalism, a much broader form of ethnic nationalism which supports Iraqi nationalism and links it to matters that impact Arabs as a whole. Saddam Hussein believed that the recognition of the ancient Mesopotamian origins and heritage of Iraqi Arabs was complementary to supporting Arab nationalism.

In the course of his reign, the Ba'athist regime officially included the historic Kurdish Muslim leader Saladin as a patriotic symbol in Iraq, while Saddam called himself son of the Babylonian King Nebuchadnezzar and had stamped the bricks of ancient Babylon with his name and titles next to him. As a sign of his consolidation of power, Saddam's personality cult pervaded Iraqi society. He had thousands of portraits, posters, statues and murals erected in his honor all over Iraq. His face could be seen on the sides of office buildings, schools, airports, and shops, as well as on Iraqi currency.

Saddam's personality cult reflected his efforts to appeal to the various elements in Iraqi society. This was seen in his variety of apparel: when visited villages, he appeared in the costumes of the Arabs, a thawb which the traditional clothes of the Arab peasant (which he essentially wore during his childhood in his village), and even Kurdish clothing, but also appeared in Western suits fitted by his favorite tailor and hat, projecting the image of a powerful leader. Sometimes he would also be portrayed as a devout Muslim, wearing full headdress and robe, praying toward Mecca.

Several Iraqi leaders, Lebanese arms merchant Sarkis Soghanalian and others have claimed that Saddam financed Chirac's party in France. In 1991 Saddam threatened to expose those who had taken largesse from him: "From Mr. Chirac to Mr. Chevènement, politicians and economic leaders were in open competition to spend time with us and flatter us. We have now grasped the reality of the situation. If the trickery continues, we will be forced to unmask them, all of them, before the French public." France armed Saddam and it was Iraq's largest trade partner throughout Saddam's rule. Seized documents show how French officials and businessmen close to Chirac, including Charles Pasqua, his former interior minister, personally benefitted from the deals with Saddam.

Because Saddam Hussein rarely left Iraq, Tariq Aziz, one of Saddam's aides, travelled abroad extensively and represented Iraq at many diplomatic meetings. In foreign affairs, Saddam sought to have Iraq play a leading role in the Middle East. Iraq signed an aid pact with the Soviet Union in 1972, and arms were sent along with several thousand advisers. The 1978 crackdown on Iraqi Communists and a shift of trade toward the West strained Iraqi relations with the Soviet Union; Iraq then took on a more Western orientation until the Gulf War in 1991.

After the oil crisis of 1973, France had changed to a more pro- Arab policy and was accordingly rewarded by Saddam with closer ties. He made a state visit to France in 1975, cementing close ties with some French business and ruling political circles. In 1975 Saddam negotiated an accord with Iran that contained Iraqi concessions on border disputes. In return, Iran agreed to stop supporting opposition Kurds in Iraq. Saddam led Arab opposition to the Camp David Accords between Egypt and Israel.

In early 1979, Iran's Shah Mohammad Reza Pahlavi was overthrown by the Islamic Revolution, thus giving way to an Islamic republic led by the Ayatollah Ruhollah

Khomeini. The influence of revolutionary Shi'ite Islam grew apace in the region, particularly in countries with large Shi'ite populations, especially Iraq. Saddam feared that radical Islamic ideas—hostile to his secular rule— were rapidly spreading inside his country among the majority Shi'ite population.

There had also been bitter enmity between Saddam and Khomeini since the 1970s. Khomeini, having been exiled from Iran in 1964, took up residence in Iraq, at the Shi'ite holy city of An Najaf. There he involved himself with Iraqi Shi'ites and developed a strong, worldwide religious and political following against the Iranian Government, which Saddam tolerated. When Khomeini began to urge the Shi'ites there to overthrow Saddam and under pressure from the Shah, who had agreed to a rapprochement between Iraq and Iran in 1975, Saddam agreed to expel Khomeini in 1978 to France. Here, Khomeini gained media connections and collaborated with a much larger Iranian community, to his advantage.

After Khomeini gained power, skirmishes between Iraq and revolutionary Iran occurred for ten months over the sovereignty of the disputed Shatt al-Arab waterway, which divides the two countries. During this period, Saddam Hussein publicly maintained that it was in Iraq's interest not to engage with Iran, and that it was in the interests of both nations to maintain peaceful relations. In a private meeting with Salah Omar al-Ali, Iraq's permanent ambassador to the United Nations, he revealed that he intended to invade and occupy a large part of Iran within months. Later, probably to appeal for support from the US and most Western nations, he would make toppling the Islamic government one of his intentions as well.

Iraq invaded Iran, first attacking Mehrabad Airport of Tehran and then entering the oil-rich Iranian land of

Khuzestan, which also has a sizable Arab minority, on the 22nd of September 1980 and declared it a new province of Iraq. With the support of the Arab states, the US, and Europe, and heavily financed by the Arab states of the Persian Gulf, Saddam Hussein had become "the defender of the Arab world" against a revolutionary Iran. The only exception was the Soviet Union, who initially refused to supply Iraq, on the basis of neutrality in the conflict, although in his memoirs, Mikhail Gorbachev claimed that Leonid Brezhnev refused to aid Saddam over infuriation of Saddam's treatment of Iraqi communists. Consequently, many viewed Iraq as "an agent of the civilized world." The blatant disregard of international law and violations of international borders were ignored. Instead, Iraq received economic and military support from its allies, who overlooked Saddam's use of chemical warfare against the Kurds and the Iranians, in addition to Iraq's efforts to develop nuclear weapons.

In the first days of the war, there was heavy ground fighting around strategic ports as Iraq launched an attack on Khuzestan.

After making some initial gains, Iraq's troops began to suffer losses from human wave attacks by Iran. By 1982, Iraq was on the defensive and looking for ways to end the war.

At this point, Saddam asked his ministers for candid advice. Health Minister Dr. Riyadh Ibrahim suggested that Saddam temporarily step down to promote peace negotiations. Initially, Saddam Hussein appeared to take in this opinion as part of his cabinet democracy. A few weeks later, Dr. Ibrahim was sacked when held responsible for a fatal incident in an Iraqi hospital where a patient died from intravenous administration of the wrong concentration of potassium supplement. Dr. Ibrahim was arrested a few days after his removal from the cabinet. He was known to have publicly declared before that arrest that he was "glad that he got away alive." Pieces of Ibrahim's dismembered body were delivered to his wife the next day.

Iraq quickly found itself bogged down in one of the longest and most destructive wars of attrition of the 20th century. During the war, Iraq used chemical weapons against Iranian forces fighting on the southern front and Kurdish separatists who were attempting to open up a northern front in Iraq with the help of Iran. These chemical weapons were developed by Iraq from materials and technology supplied primarily by West German companies as well as using dual-use technology imported following the Reagan administration's lifting of export restrictions. The US government also supplied Iraq with "satellite photos showing Iranian deployments." In a US bid to open full diplomatic relations with Iraq, the country was removed from the US list of State Sponsors of Terrorism. Ostensibly, this was because of improvement in the regime's record, although former US Assistant Secretary of Defense Noel Koch later stated, "No one had any doubts about the Iraqis' continued involvement in terrorism ... The real reason was to help them succeed in the war against Iran." The Soviet Union, France, and China together accounted for over ninety percent of the value of Iraq's arms imports between 1980 and 1988.

Saddam reached out to other Arab governments for cash and political support during the war, particularly after Iraq's oil industry severely suffered at the hands of the Iranian navy in the Persian Gulf. Iraq successfully gained some military and financial aid, as well as diplomatic and moral support, from the Soviet Union, China, France, and the US, which together feared the prospects of the expansion of revolutionary Iran's influence in the region. The Iranians, demanding that the international community should force Iraq to pay war reparations to Iran, refused any suggestions for a cease-fire. Despite several calls for a ceasefire by the United Nations Security Council, hostilities continued until the 20th of August 1988.

On the 16th of March 1988, the Kurdish town of Halabja was attacked with a mix of mustard gas and nerve agents, killing five thousand civilians, and maiming, disfiguring, or seriously debilitating ten thousand more. The attack occurred in conjunction with the 1988 al-Anfal Campaign designed to reassert central control of the mostly Kurdish population of areas of northern Iraq and defeat the Kurdish peshmerga rebel forces. Claims by Saddam's government and its international supporters that Iran had actually gassed the Kurds at Halabja have been thoroughly debunked. .

The bloody eight-year war ended in a stalemate. Neither side had achieved what they had originally desired and the borders were left nearly unchanged. The southern, oil rich and prosperous Khuzestan and Basra area, the main focus of the war, and the primary source of their economies were almost completely destroyed and were left at the pre-1979 border, while Iran managed to make some small gains on its borders in the Northern Kurdish area. Both economies, previously healthy and expanding, were left in ruins.

Saddam borrowed tens of billions of dollars from other Arab states and a few billions from elsewhere during the 1980s to fight Iran, mainly to prevent the expansion of Shi'a radicalism. This backfired on Iraq and the Arab states, for Khomeini was widely perceived as a hero for managing to defend Iran and maintain the war with little foreign support against the heavily backed Iraq and only managed to boost Islamic radicalism not only within the Arab states, but within Iraq itself, creating new tensions between the Sunni Ba'ath Party and the majority Shi'a population. Faced with rebuilding Iraq's infrastructure and internal resistance, Saddam desperately re-sought cash, this time for post-war reconstruction.

The end of the war with Iran served to deepen latent tensions between Iraq and its wealthy neighbour Kuwait. Saddam urged the Kuwaitis to waive the Iraqi debt accumulated in the war, some thirty billion dollars, but they refused. Saddam pushed oil- exporting countries to raise oil prices by cutting back production; Kuwait refused, then led the opposition in OPEC to the cuts that Saddam had requested. Kuwait was pumping large amounts of oil, and thus keeping prices low, when Iraq needed to sell high-priced oil from its wells to pay off its huge debt.

Saddam had consistently argued that Kuwait had historically been an integral part of Iraq, and had only come into being as a result of interference from the British government; echoing a belief that Iraqi nationalists had supported for the past fifty years. This belief was one of the few articles of faith uniting the political scene in a nation rife with sharp social, ethnic, religious, and ideological divides. The extent of Kuwaiti oil reserves also intensified tensions in the region. The oil reserves of Kuwait, with a population of two million next to Iraq's twenty-five were roughly equal to those of Iraq. Taken together, Iraq and Kuwait sat on top of some twenty percent of the world's known oil reserves; Saudi Arabia held another twenty-five percent. Saddam still had an experienced and well-equipped army, which he used to influence regional affairs. He later ordered troops to the Iraq – Kuwait border.

As Iraqi and Kuwaiti relations rapidly deteriorated, Saddam was receiving conflicting information about how the US would respond to the prospects of an invasion. For one, Washington had been taking measures to cultivate a constructive relationship with Iraq for roughly a decade. The Reagan administration gave Iraq roughly four billion dollars in agricultural credits to bolster it against Iran. Saddam's Iraq became "the third-largest recipient of US assistance."

Reacting to Western criticism in April 1990, Saddam threatened to destroy half of Israel with chemical weapons if it moved against Iraq. In May 1990 he criticized US support for Israel warning that the US cannot maintain such a policy while professing friendship towards the Arabs. In July 1990 he threatened force against Kuwait and the UAE saying "The policies of some Arab rulers are American They are inspired by America to undermine Arab interests and security." The US sent warplanes and combat ships to the Persian Gulf in response to these threats.

US officials attempted to maintain a conciliatory line with Iraq, indicating that while George H. W. Bush and James Baker did not want force used, they would not take any position on the Iraq– Kuwait boundary dispute and did not want to become involved. Later, Iraqi and Kuwaiit officials met for a final negotiation session, which failed. Saddam then sent his troops into Kuwait. As tensions between Washington and Saddam began to escalate, the Soviet Union, under Mikhail Gorbachev, strengthened its military relationship with the Iraqi leader, providing him military advisers, arms and aid.   .

On the 2nd of August 1990, Saddam's forces invaded Kuwait, initially claiming assistance to "Kuwaiti revolutionaries," thus sparking an international crisis. On the 4th of August an Iraqi- backed "Provisional Government of Free Kuwait" was proclaimed, but a total lack of legitimacy and support for it led to an   8th of August announcement of a "merger" of the two countries. On the 28th of August Kuwait formally became the 19th Governorate of Iraq. Just two years after the 1988 Iraq and Iran truce, Saddam Hussein did what his Gulf patrons had earlier paid him to prevent. Having removed the threat of Iranian fundamentalism he overran Kuwait and confronted his Gulf neighbours in the name of Arab nationalism and Islam.

When later asked why he invaded Kuwait, Saddam first claimed that it was because Kuwait was rightfully Iraq's 19th province and then said "When I get something into my head I act. That's just the way I am." Saddam Hussein could pursue such military aggression with a "military machine paid for in large part by the tens of billions of dollars Kuwait and the Gulf states had poured into Iraq and the weapons and technology provided by the Soviet Union, Germany, and France." It was revealed during his 2003-2004 interrogation that in addition to economic disputes, an insulting exchange between the Kuwaiti emir Al Sabah and the Iraqi foreign minister - during which Saddam claimed that the emir stated his intention to turn every Iraqi woman into a ten dollar prostitute by ruining Iraq financially – and this was a decisive factor in triggering the Iraqi invasion.

US President George H. W. Bush responded cautiously for the first several days. On one hand, Kuwait, prior to this point, had been a virulent enemy of Israel and was the Persian Gulf monarchy that had the friendliest relations with the Soviets. On the other hand, Washington foreign policymakers, along with Middle East experts, military critics, and firms heavily invested in the region, were extremely concerned with stability in this region. The invasion immediately triggered fears that the world's price of oil, and therefore control of the world economy, was at stake. Britain profited heavily from billions of dollars of Kuwaiti investments and bank deposits. Bush was perhaps swayed while meeting with British prime minister Margaret Thatcher, who happened to be in America at the time.

Cooperation between the US and the Soviet Union made possible the passage of resolutions in the United Nations Security Council (UNSC) giving Iraq a deadline to leave Kuwait and approving the use of force if Saddam did not comply with the timetable. US officials feared Iraqi retaliation against oil-rich Saudi Arabia, since the 1940s a close ally of Washington, for the Saudis' opposition to the invasion of Kuwait. Accordingly, the US and a group of allies, including countries as diverse as Egypt, Syria and Czechoslovakia, deployed a massive number of troops along the Saudi border with Kuwait and Iraq in order to encircle the Iraqi army, the largest in the Middle East.

During the period of negotiations and threats following the invasion, Saddam focused renewed attention on the Palestinian problem by promising to withdraw his forces from Kuwait if Israel would relinquish the occupied territories in the West Bank, the Golan Heights, and the Gaza Strip. Saddam's proposal further split the Arab world, pitting US- and Western-supported Arab states against the Palestinians. The allies ultimately rejected any linkage between the Kuwait crisis and Palestinian issues.

Saddam ignored the Security Council deadline. Backed by the Security Council, a US-led coalition launched round-the-clock missile and aerial attacks on Iraq, beginning on the 16th of January 1991. Israel, though subjected to attack by Iraqi missiles, refrained from retaliating in order not to provoke Arab states into leaving the coalition. A ground force consisting largely of US and British armored and infantry divisions ejected Saddam's army from Kuwait in February 1991 and occupied the southern portion of Iraq as far as the Euphrates.

In the end, the Iraqi army proved unable to compete on the battlefield with the highly mobile coalition land forces and their overpowering air support. Some one hundred and seventy five thousand Iraqis were taken prisoner and casualties were estimated at over eighty five thousand. As part of the cease-fire agreement, Iraq agreed to scrap all poison gas and germ weapons and allow UN observers to inspect the sites. UN trade sanctions would remain in effect until Iraq complied with all terms. Saddam publicly claimed victory at the end of the war.

Iraq's ethnic and religious divisions, together with the brutality of the conflict that this had engendered, laid the groundwork for post-war rebellions. In the aftermath of the fighting, social and ethnic unrest among Shi'ite Muslims, Kurds, and dissident military units threatened the stability of Saddam's government. Uprisings erupted in the Kurdish north and Shi'a southern and central parts of Iraq, but were ruthlessly repressed. Uprisings in 1991 led to the deaths of between one hundred and one hundred and eighty thousand people, mostly civilians.

The US, which had urged Iraqis to rise up against Saddam, did nothing to assist the rebellions. The Iranians, despite the widespread Shi'ite rebellions, had no interest in provoking another war, while Turkey opposed any prospect of Kurdish independence, and the Saudis and other conservative Arab states feared an Iran-style Shi'ite revolution. Saddam, having survived the immediate crisis in the wake of defeat, was left firmly in control of Iraq, although the country never recovered either economically or militarily from the Gulf War.

Saddam routinely cited his survival as "proof" that Iraq had in fact won the war against the US. This message earned Saddam a great deal of popularity in many sectors of the Arab world. John Esposito wrote, "Arabs and Muslims were pulled in two directions. That they rallied not so much to Saddam Hussein as to the bipolar nature of the confrontation (the West versus the Arab Muslim world) and the issues that Saddam proclaimed: Arab unity, self-sufficiency, and social justice." As a result, Saddam Hussein appealed to many people for the same reasons that attracted more and more followers to Islamic revivalism and also for the same reasons that fuelled anti- Western feelings.

The United Nations-placed sanctions against Iraq for invading Kuwait were not lifted, blocking Iraqi oil exports. During the late 1990s, the UN considered relaxing the sanctions imposed because of the hardships suffered by ordinary Iraqis. Studies dispute the number of people who died in south and central Iraq during the years of the sanctions. On the 9th of December 1996, Saddam's government accepted the Oil-for-Food Programme that the UN had first offered in 1992.

Relations between the US and Iraq remained tense following the Gulf War. The US launched a missile attack aimed at Iraq's intelligence headquarters in Baghdad the 26th of June 1993, citing evidence of repeated Iraqi violations of the "no fly zones" imposed after the Gulf War and for incursions into Kuwait. US officials continued to accuse Saddam of violating the terms of the Gulf War's cease fire, by developing weapons of mass destruction and other banned weaponry, and violating the UN- imposed sanctions. Also during the 1990s, President Bill Clinton maintained sanctions and ordered air strikes in the "Iraqi no-fly zones" (Operation Desert Fox), in the hope that Saddam would be overthrown by political enemies inside Iraq. Western charges of Iraqi resistance to UN access to suspected weapons were the pretext for crises between 1997 and 1998, culminating in intensive US and British missile strikes on Iraq, 16–19 December 1998. After two years of intermittent activity, US and British warplanes struck harder at sites near Baghdad in February 2001

Saddam continued involvement in politics abroad. Video tapes retrieved after show his intelligence chiefs meeting with Arab journalists, including a meeting with the former managing director of Al-Jazeera, Mohammed Jassem al-Ali, in 2000. In the video Saddam's son Uday advised al-Ali about hires in Al-Jazeera: "During your last visit here along with your colleagues we talked about a number of issues, and it does appear that you indeed were listening to what I was saying since changes took place and new faces came on board such as that lad, Mansour." He was later sacked by Al-Jazeera.

Many members of the international community, especially the US, continued to view Saddam as a bellicose tyrant who was a threat to the stability of the region. In his January 2002 state of the union address to Congress, President George W. Bush spoke of an "axis of evil" consisting of Iran, North Korea, and Iraq. Moreover, Bush announced that he would possibly take action to topple the Iraqi government, because of the threat of its weapons of mass destruction. Bush stated that "The Iraqi regime has plotted to develop anthrax, and nerve gas, and nuclear weapons for over a decade ... Iraq continues to flaunt its hostility toward America and to support terror."

After the passing of UNSC Resolution 1441, which demanded that Iraq give "immediate, unconditional and active cooperation" with UN and IAEA inspections, Saddam allowed U.N. weapons inspectors led by Hans Blix to return to Iraq. During the renewed inspections beginning in November 2002, Blix found no stockpiles of WMD and noted the "proactive" but not always "immediate" Iraqi cooperation as called for by Resolution 1441. With war still looming on the 24th of February 2003, Saddam took part in an interview with CBS News reporter Dan Rather. Talking for more than three hours, he denied possessing any weapons of mass destruction, or any other weapons prohibited by UN guidelines. He also expressed a wish to have a live televised debate with George W. Bush, which was declined. It was his first interview with a US reporter in over a decade. CBS aired the taped interview later that week. Saddam later told an FBI interviewer that he once left open the possibility that Iraq possessed weapons of mass destruction in order to appear strong against Iran.

The Iraqi government and military collapsed within three weeks of the beginning of the US-led 2003 invasion of Iraq on the 20th of March. By the beginning of April, US-led forces occupied much of Iraq. The resistance of the much-weakened Iraqi Army either crumbled or shifted to guerrilla tactics, and it appeared that Saddam had lost control of Iraq. He was last seen in a video which purported to show him in the Baghdad suburbs surrounded by supporters. When Baghdad fell to US-led forces on 9 April, marked symbolically by the toppling of his statue, Saddam was nowhere to be found.

In April 2003, Saddam's whereabouts remained in question during the weeks following the fall of Baghdad and the conclusion of the major fighting of the war. Various sightings of Saddam were reported in the weeks following the war, but none was authenticated. At various times Saddam released audio tapes promoting popular resistance to his ousting. Saddam was placed at the top of the "US list of most-wanted Iraqis." In July 2003, his sons Uday and Qusay and his fourteen-year-old grandson Mustapha were killed in a three-hour gunfight with US forces.

On the 13th of December 2003, in Operation Red
Dawn, Saddam was captured by American forces after
being found hiding in a hole in the ground near a farmhouse in ad-Dawr, near Tikrit. Following his capture, Saddam was transported to a US base near Tikrit, and later
taken to the American base near Baghdad. Documents
obtained and released by the National Security Archive
detail FBI interviews and conversations with Saddam
while he was in US custody. On the 14th of December, US
administrator in Iraq Paul Bremer confirmed that Saddam
Hussein had indeed been captured at a farmhouse in ad-
Dawr near Tikrit. Bremer presented video footage of Saddam in custody.

Saddam was shown with a full beard and hair longer
than his familiar appearance. He was described by US officials as being in good health. Bremer reported plans to put
Saddam on trial, but claimed that the details of such a trial
had not yet been determined. Iraqis and Americans who
spoke with Saddam after his capture generally reported
that he remained self-assured, describing himself as a
"firm, but just leader."

British tabloid newspaper The Sun posted a picture of
Saddam wearing white briefs on the front cover of a newspaper. Other photographs inside the paper show Saddam
washing his trousers, shuffling, and sleeping. The US government stated that it considered the release of the pictures
a violation of the Geneva Convention, and that it would
investigate the photographs.

The guards at the Baghdad detention facility called
their prisoner "Vic," which stands for 'Very Important
Criminal', and let him plant a small garden near his cell.
The nickname and the garden are among the details about
the former Iraqi leader that emerged during a March 2008
tour of the Baghdad prison and cell where Saddam slept,

bathed, and kept a journal and wrote poetry in the final days before his execution; he was concerned to ensure his legacy and how the history would be told. The tour was conducted by US Marine Maj. Gen. Doug Stone, overseer of detention operations for the US military in Iraq at the time. During his imprisonment he exercised and was allowed to have his personal garden, he also smoked his cigars and wrote his diary in the courtyard of his cell.

On the 30th of June 2004, Saddam, held in custody by US forces at the US base "Camp Cropper," along with eleven other senior Ba'athist leaders, were handed over to the interim Iraqi government to stand trial for crimes against humanity and other offences.

A few weeks later, Saddam was charged by the Iraqi Special Tribunal with crimes committed against residents of Dujail in 1982, following a failed assassination attempt against him. Specific charges included the murder of one hundred and forty- eight people, torture of women and children and the illegal arrest of three hundred and ninety-nine others.

On the 5th of November 2006, Saddam was found guilty of crimes against humanity and sentenced to death by hanging. Saddam's half-brother, Barzan Ibrahim, and Awad Hamed al- Bandar, head of Iraq's Revolutionary Court in 1982, were convicted of similar charges. The verdict and sentencing were oth appealed, but subsequently affirmed by Iraq's Supreme Court of Appeals.

Saddam was hanged on the first day of Eid ul-Adha, the 30th of December 2006, despite his wish to be executed by firing squad. The execution was carried out at Camp Justice, an Iraqi army base in Kadhimiya, an area of northeast Baghdad.

Saddam's last words during the execution, "May God's blessings be upon Muhammad and his household. And may God hasten their appearance and curse their enemies."

Saddam was buried at his birthplace of Al-Awja in Tikrit, Iraq, on the 31st of December 2006. His tomb was reported to have been destroyed in March 2015 but before it was destroyed, a Sunni tribal group reportedly removed his body to a secret location.